MW01120249

Writing from the Margins

Writing from the Margins

Exploring the Writing Practices of Youth in the Juvenile Justice System

Kristine E. Pytash

ROWMAN & LITTLEFIELD
Lanham • Boulder • New York • London

Published by Rowman & Littlefield
A wholly owned subsidiary of The Rowman & Littlefield Publishing Group, Inc.
4501 Forbes Boulevard, Suite 200, Lanham, Maryland 20706
www.rowman.com

Unit A, Whitacre Mews, 26-34 Stannary Street, London SE11 4AB

British Library Cataloguing in Publication Information Available

Library of Congress Cataloging-in-Publication Data Available

ISBN: 978-1-4758-3063-7 (cloth : alk. paper)
ISBN: 978-1-4758-3064-4 (pbk : alk. paper)
ISBN: 978-1-4758-3065-1 (electronic)

Printed in the United States of America

Contents

Acknowledgments

Gregory Boyle, founder of Homeboy Industries, in a sermon describing his work with former gang members, says, "We brace ourselves because people will accuse us of wasting our time, but the prophet Jeremiah writes, 'of in this place of which you say it is a waste, there will be heard again the voice of mirth, the voices of those who sing' and so let us make those voices heard."

Juvenile detention centers are places that society often views as a "waste," and yet the youth in these spaces are yearning for their voices to be understood and valued. It is crucial that we listen to them, and this book is an attempt to relay the stories of young people whose voices are often forgotten, ignored, and pushed to the margins of our society.

Many people have supported my voice throughout the process of writing this book. I am blessed to have wonderful friends who continually supported me throughout the writing process. I appreciate all the times they asked about how the book was coming along and their words of encouragement. Courtney, Deanna, Jen, Jenny, and Caitlin—thank you. Joey, David, and Mike—thank you for your continuous support of my research and of the writing of this book.

I am deeply appreciative of the judges and detention center staff—superintendents and guards—who have allowed me to work in their facilities. Thank you for trusting me and for seeing the value in my research and teaching. Thank you to the teachers who graciously allowed me to document their teaching and also allowed me to teach in their classrooms. In order to keep anonymity, I cannot include names; however, their role in my work is invaluable. I have learned an incredible amount from watching them teach and talking to them about teaching.

I have been blessed with wonderful colleagues, who I met at Kent State University through professional organizations and who not only provided support and encouragement but were also willing to read chapters and give feedback: Trish Crawford, Bob Fecho, Rachel Karmcher-Klein, Mellinee Lesley, Ian O'Byrne, Mike Manderino, Tim Rasinski, Ryan Rish, and Phil Wilder—thank you!

I would like to thank my editor, Sarah Jubar, for her editorial assistance, guidance, and patience.

I am fortunate that my work as a teacher educator is in the Adolescent and Adult Education Program at Kent State University. My colleagues are devoted scholars and educators committed to preparing teachers in ways that promote equity in educational spaces. Joanne Caniglia, Joanne Dowdy, Todd Hawley, Lisa Borgerding, and Walter Gershon—thank you for the many ways you support my work. In particular, I am thankful to codirect the Integrated Language Arts Program with Bill Kist, who consistently supports my work at the detention center and since the first day we met has encouraged me to write this book. His feedback on my proposal and early versions of chapters was invaluable.

Lisa Testa, a member of ADED and a teacher educator in the INLA program, is a colleague, close friend, and lately a trusted companion in developing programs for preservice teachers and new initiatives for detained youth. I have learned so much from watching her teach and seeing how she approaches all students with kindness. I have benefited from our many conversations, which have been vital in helping me think deeply about writing and writing pedagogy.

I owe a debt of gratitude to Rick Ferdig, a mentor and friend, who is always generous with his time and knowledge. He has supported my research by asking me difficult questions, helping me to explore new ideas, and encouraging me to move beyond the status quo. Rick spent an incredible amount of time helping me think through the organization of this book and providing feedback throughout the entire writing process. I cannot thank him enough for all the ways he has guided and supported my scholarship.

This book truly would not be possible without my parents' unwavering support and love. I come from generations of teachers, and my mom is surely the greatest teacher I have ever known. She has always been a teacher for students without a voice and has fought many battles for her students so that they had the opportunity to receive an excellent education. She is truly the most compassionate, kind, and generous person I know. The greatest compliment I receive is when people tell me "You are so much like your mom."

As with all of my scholarship and writing, my dad is interested in my work and enjoys engaging in debate and discussion. He is incredibly thoughtful and analytical, inspiring me to think critically and write with purpose. He challenges and encourages me with abundant amounts of love. And throughout the writing of this book, both my mom and dad have read multiple drafts and provided feedback, all the while being wonderful grandparents to JJ, Ryan, and Bryce—spending time with them so I could sneak in extra writing sessions.

Finally, and most importantly, I am deeply indebted to the young adults I have met over the last seven years. Thank you for trusting me with your stories, words, and voices.

Introduction

Why Are You Here?

NEVEAH

Neveah is a quiet 13-year-old Caucasian female with long brown hair. She is so soft-spoken that I often have to ask her to repeat herself when we talk. On this particular day, I ask her to write a literacy vignette, a narrative piece about a time when reading and writing were important in her life. She rubs her very pregnant belly as she contemplates her topic.

Over the course of the year, Neveah shared selections of her poetry with me, and from this I knew that her poetry was intricately connected to her life. She often chose to write about her unborn baby, her boyfriend, or her sisters, and because she is between foster-care homes, I expect her to write her vignette about one of those closest to her.

On this day, however, she tells me a new story, relating how her mom wrote her poems. As Neveah reflects that she is on the brink of motherhood, she settles on writing about the first time she read a poem her mom had written for her.

DESIREE

Desiree is a 17-year-old black female who in a few short months will be transferred from the detention center where I facilitate a writing group to a women's prison, where she will spend the next 20 years of her life. I became acquainted with Desiree as a writer during the time she participated in the group.

> "My little Angel"
>
> Once when i was a years old me and my mom got into an argument and i felt as if i was alone and she diddent care about me like she used to.
> So i started to go through some old photo albums of when i was 3 years-old, after going through all of them i found this tiny, little, worn out book, looking through it, i realized it was my moms old poetry book on the 11th page was the most amazing poem i had ever heard, it was called "My little Angel".
> While reading it tears came streaming down my face and all i could hear was the hateful words i had said to her, but all she could say was "your still my little angel, and i love you". suddenly i realized she always was there, she poured out her soul and gave it to me in simple little words. In reality that was all it took. My mom has always been there for me and im always trying to stay as her little angel. And to this day i'll never forget what she has lost and what she's givin up, all for me. i love her and im still

Neveah's vignette about her mom's poem, "My Little Angel"

   During a lesson on concrete poetry, Desiree writes a poem titled "Wall." When asked about the inspiration for the poem, she explains, "The brick wall—all the heartache in my life—needs to be torn down." After explaining her poem, I ask Desiree why she and others write in the detention center. She responds, "We're just looking for someone to hear us, to understand us. We're just looking for someone to accept us."

PAUL

Paul, 17, is a Caucasian male who has just been released from a detention center and is now attending an alternative school. He begins to tell me about his favorite book, a book he read in the detention center.

> *Paul: The book was* The Star-Spangled Secret. *It was back when the British war was going on. This little girl, like 13 or 14, and her brother always liked boats. And he was working on a boat, and the captain was working for the British. And they didn't know it until then, so they tied him up and threw him overboard. And they thought he died, but he actually lived. So the whole story she's looking for him.*

> *Kristine: Do you know if she found him?*

> *Paul: I'm not sure. I didn't finish the book. Actually, is there any chance you could find that book for me so I can finish it?*

That afternoon I rummage through the detention center's library, which consists of two metal carts. No librarian, no bookshelves, just approximately 150 books stacked haphazardly. Flipping through pages of books, I am guided only by Paul's description as I skim pages, searching for the specific storyline. Later I type descriptions and keywords into Google, hoping the Internet will point me toward the book. I ask librarians and colleagues, but I can't find Paul's book.

I tell Paul that I cannot find this particular book for him, but I come with additional book recommendations. Paul looks downhearted and explains that finding and reading the entire book is important. Not only does he truly want to know the ending, but he also tells me that the youth at the detention center believe that if they start reading a book but don't finish it, they will return to jail. Paul unfortunately did not have the chance to finish the book and believes there is a significant possibility he will return to the detention center in the future.

* * *

Neveah, Paul, and Desiree's stories represent hope. Neveah hopes that she will be a good mother to her unborn baby. Paul hopes that he will not be faced with returning to the detention center. And Desiree hopes that one day someone will hear, understand, and accept her. Neveah, Paul, and Desiree all ardently wish for their lives to improve—and reading and writing became pathways for fulfilling this wish.

For the past seven years, I have worked closely with young adults who have been suspended and expelled from school, often relegated to alternative schools and juvenile detention centers. I have met hundreds of young adults who occupy these spaces, and while they and their stories are unique, a theme emerges: the role of reading and writing in their lives.

I use Fecho's (2003) term *practitioner researcher* to describe my role as a teacher educator and researcher. As a practitioner researcher, I have conducted various studies in which I systematically examined the role of reading and writing in youths' lives. I have studied instructional practices for the teaching of writing in juvenile detention facilities, and I have investigated preservice teacher learning of writing instruction when conducting field-based experiences in juvenile detention centers.

In addition, I have facilitated a weekly writing workshop in a juvenile detention facility for more than four years. Therefore, this book is a way to share what I have learned by featuring the projects, personal stories, and writings of the young adults I have worked with over the past seven years. It is my hope that sharing their stories, their writing, and ultimately what I have learned will both provide a voice for their experiences and help us to understand the role of writing in their lives.

I have three goals for this book. The first goal is to review the current research on writing instruction and consider a framework for teaching writing. The second goal is to provide an examination of the writing practices that youth are doing in their personal lives. And the third goal is to debunk the myth of what it means to be a "struggling" writer by looking at what happens when youth in juvenile detention facilities are provided with ambitious literacy instruction.

Finally, I hope all teachers—particularly those who work with marginalized and often forgotten youth—will consider the meaning of equity in education and how ambitious writing instruction can disrupt the school-to-prison pipeline.

These goals are met by providing close-up accounts of the writing practices that help youth cope with their life events; those key practices that allow them to voice their experiences; and especially the reading and writing experiences that provide hope for their futures, dreams, and aspirations. Not only are these accounts valuable for recognizing the importance of youths' writing practices, but also each account holds implications for the ways we engage youth in writing instruction.

THROWAWAY KIDS

In every school are young adults in chaos. They might be the adolescents who act defiantly or are hostile when asked to follow a teacher's seemingly neutral set of directions. They might be the youth who exhibit escape behaviors, such as not attending school or not completing work while in school. They might be the young adults who fight or act out violently. Adolescents who experience chaos are often living in circumstances that overwhelm them—and also overwhelm the adults in their lives who are trying to figure out solutions to such complicated issues as hunger, homelessness, abuse, and neglect.

The rhetoric surrounding these youths tends to be that they are "throwaways," without any worth in their lives. It is easy to ignore them and to move them to other spaces, such as "bad" schools, alternative schools, or detention centers, so that their complicated issues can be evaded. This was evident to me when my local newspaper ran an article with the headline "Normalcy Returns After Mass Exodus of Students." The article praised the school administration for the decision to get rid of adolescents they described as "bad," "troubled," and "problem students." The implication was that school districts would have "good" schools simply by eliminating certain students.

This trend is what educators, researchers, and scholars refer to as the school-to-prison pipeline. Many scholars, however, argue that this oversimplifies how schools fail students and glosses over the fact that schools frequently reproduce inequities and sustain political structures built on segregation, racism, and classism.

In addition, the term *school-to-prison pipeline* gives the impression that what happens or doesn't happen within a traditional K–12 district catapults students into the juvenile justice system. This focuses our attention on schools instead of also considering all the other spaces where youth are educated, such as community-based after-school programs, alternative schools, charter schools, online and virtual schools, juvenile detention facilities, and youth prisons. We need to consider how all of these entities and the services youth receive influence their lives.

Finally, the underlying assumption about students trapped in the school-to-prison pipeline is that they struggle academically. This, however, oversimplifies how adolescents engage in literacy and fails to recognize that reading and writing are central pursuits for many of the youth who are suspended, expelled, and sent to alternative schools and juvenile detention centers. In a disordered and uncontrollable world, reading and writing can provide adolescents an escape to gain a sense of control over their lives. Many people, including teachers, overlook the role of reading and writing in these spaces and believe that young adults are not passionate readers and writers.

This book is dedicated to recognizing and discovering the deeply personal and intense ways young adults engage in reading and writing in these particular spaces.

BEHIND BARS

Since the early 1990s, juvenile crime rates have decreased, and yet various factors and federal policies (e.g., the Zero Tolerance Act) have increased the number of young adults in juvenile detention facilities (Chesney-Lind & Shelden, 2004; Holman & Ziedenberg, 2006; Krisberg, 2005). Today, even though juvenile crime has decreased, approximately 500,000 young adults are detained, and police arrest nearly 1.5 million juveniles each year (Office of Juvenile Justice and Delinquency Prevention: Snyder & Sickmund, 1999).

Many troubling statistics are associated with the juvenile justice system. Bernstein (2014) writes, "[J]uvenile incarceration is also one of the most glaring examples of racial injustice our nation has to offer" (p. 8), as it is well documented that there is an overrepresentation of males of color throughout the juvenile justice system (Foley, 2001; Leiber & Fox, 2005; Noguera, 2003; Snyder & Sickmund, 1999; Wordes, Bynum, & Corley, 1994; Wordes & Jones, 1998).

According to Brinkley-Rubinstein, Craven, & McCormack (2014), while "African Americans account for only about 16% of the total number of adolescents in the United States, they represent over 70% of the youth who are involved in school-related arrests and make up nearly 40% of the total youth currently imprisoned" (p. 25). This overrepresentation is referred to as disproportionate minority contact (DMC). Efforts have been made to reduce the number of youths of color involved in the juvenile justice system, including the 2002 Juvenile Justice and Delinquency Prevention Act (juvjustice.org). However, young men of color from marginalized backgrounds are still more likely to be arrested and charged and receive harsher sentences in juvenile courts (Brinkley-Rubinstein, Craven, & McCormack, 2014; Leiber & Fox, 2005; Noguera, 2003). Furthermore, they are more likely to return to jail.

Researchers have documented a "nearly 50% increase" in girls in the juvenile justice system, "with girls accounting for 29% of all juvenile arrests" (Leve, Chamberlain, & Kim, 2015). Sociologists note that "status offenses" are one of the distinguishing characteristics of female involvement in the juvenile justice system. A status offense is nonviolent or nonharmful, such as curfew violation, running away, or prostitution. Girls are more likely to be arrested for running away and prostitution, charges often associated with negative home environments. Numerous studies conclude that girls involved in the juvenile justice system are likely to be victims of abuse, particularly physical and sexual abuse (Leve, Chamberlain, & Kim, 2015); Moore, Gaskin, & Indig, 2013). In fact, Chesney-Lind and Shelden (2004) describe these girls as "in flight from sexual victimization at home" (p. 41).

Running away from home often triggers a cycle of involvement in the juvenile justice system because doing so increases the odds "of serious, violent, and chronic offending" (Leve, Chamberlain, & Kim, 2015). Young female offenses that are violent and person to person tend to be issues of family and domestic violence (Chesney-Lind & Shelden, 2004). In addition, girls exposed to child abuse or domestic violence are seven times more likely to commit a violent act.

These statistics paint a complicated portrait of youths' involvement in the juvenile justice system, as we begin to realize that these youths are also victims of violence, abuse, prejudice, and societal maltreatment. Recognizing this complexity dispels notions of youths as predators and the juvenile justice system as protecting communities from violent offenders. This is even more complex considering that anywhere from 50 to 75% of youths in detention centers have diagnosable mental illness (Liss, 2005) and all too often lack the help and counseling they need.

While being incarcerated is in and of itself an obvious negative and traumatic experience, involvement in the juvenile justice system generates long-lasting consequences. Being incarcerated or detained influences young adults' school completion rates and recidivism rates, or the likelihood that they will be rearrested, convicted, and returned to prison (Holman & Ziedenberg, 2006; Krisberg, 2005). Leve, Chamberlain, & Kim (2015) note that only 12% of youths involved in the juvenile justice system receive their high school diplomas or GEDs as young adults, influencing their ability to gain employment (Holman & Ziedenberg, 2006; Krisberg, 2005).

The results of these studies indicate that incarceration and detention do not improve public safety but rather guarantee that youths who are arrested and detained are more likely to cycle in and out of the courts and penal system. In fact, the Arkansas Division of Youth services found the "experience of incarceration is the most significant factor in increasing the odds of recidivism" (Holman & Ziedenberg, 2006, p. 4). Despite the fact that youth confinement and involvement in the juvenile justice system is a societal issue, these young adults are often overlooked and are often nonwhite, poor, and increasingly female.

THE STORIES IN THIS BOOK

In this book, youth from one jail-based alternative school and two juvenile detention facilities are featured. Their stories are derived from research conducted over the past seven years. Some of the stories come from early work following six girls as they navigated various educational spaces. Other stories come from research projects in detention centers while working with teachers to integrate instructional approaches for writing. Stories also come from my interactions with youths whom I met during my writing group at a local detention center and while facilitating a writing workshop with detained youths and preservice teachers.

Prior to conducting all of my research, informed consent was obtained from the parents, guardians, and most importantly from the youths who participated in each writing project. I am cognizant of the fact that the youths I work with are vulnerable. Being expelled, suspended, arrested, and detained has grave consequences. I also recognize the seriousness of protecting the identities of court-involved youths. In this book, I ensure confidentiality by using pseudonyms and removing information that might reveal identities.

Jail-based alternative schools are typically schools for students who have been suspended or expelled from school. These schools operate similarly to traditional schools in that students attend only during the school day; however, they are usually punitive in nature and are focused on remediating certain behaviors. Juvenile detention facilities are short-term placements for pre-adjudicated youths who have been charged with crimes and are awaiting sentencing. They also house postadjudicated youths who have been charged with crimes and are completing short-term sentences.

Most juvenile detention centers hold students for as long as 90 days, although there are instances of a youth being held for as short as 1 hour. This is dependent on the youth's criminal history, the charge, and the court's process. While in juvenile detention centers, youths are required to attend school and receive educational services. Detention centers often offer additional services, such as counseling, religious events, health classes, and writing groups, such as those I have facilitated.

Alexander County has both an alternative school and a detention center, which are located in a rural region. During the time I was working in this facility, there were 561 youths admitted to the detention center. Of the 561, 25% were female, 75% were male, 62% were reported as Caucasian, 26% were reported as African American, and 12% were reported as "other."

The second facility, Adams County Detention Center, is located in an urban region. During the time I was working in this facility, there were 1,017 youths detained. There were 320 females (31.5%) and 697 (68.5%) males. According to detention center records, of the females, 55% were African American, 34% were Caucasian, 10% were biracial, 0.5% were Asian, and 0.5% were Native American. Of the males, 61% were African American; 31% were Caucasian; 6% were biracial; 1% were Asian; and 1% were a combination of Hispanic, Native American, and Hawaiian or Pacific Islander.

Despite the differences in the geography and youth populations of these facilities, the reasons, the content, and the meanings of stories of are similar. What they write, why they write, and what they think writing accomplishes create meaningful patterns. I have worked closely with youths, facilitating writing groups and workshops in these spaces. Therefore, in addition to examining the writing practices of youth in this setting, I share stories of facilitating writing groups with youths in juvenile detention centers. Finally, Adams County houses the detention facility where I ask preservice teachers to accompany me during their field experiences.

When we come to know youths, we have the opportunity to learn not only what and how they write but also their lived experiences, encompassing what is important in their lives and how they use writing to establish and maintain their identities. Understanding who youths are and why they write allows us to better consider how to enable learning in this complex environment. And as educators, when we align ourselves with youths in these spaces, we become more aware of the social issues in their lives and classrooms.

WHAT IS LITERACY?

Education has been touted as both the problem and the solution to youth incarceration (Sander, Patall, Amoscato, Fisher, & Funk, 2012). Educators have investigated youths' reading abilities and found that incarcerated youths are typically two years behind their peers in reading (Drakeford, 2002; Foley, 2001; Harris, Baltodano, Bal, Jolivette, & Malcahy, 2009; Houchins, Jollvette, Krezmien, & Baltodano, 2008; Malmgren & Leone, 2000; Rogers-Adkinson, Melloy, Stuart, Fletcher, & Rinaldi, 2008; Vacca, 2008). This gap in literacy skills prompted research to find successful interventions like skills-based reading programs, such as the Corrective Reading Program. This research emphasizes that schools are failing certain students, namely minority males and youths in poverty.

These are the same students who are being detained, confined, and imprisoned more than any other juveniles in the United States. But this research also begs the question, What does it mean to be a *reader* and a *writer*? The dominant view of court-involved youths is that they are illiterate or at best struggling readers and writers.

The problem with focusing on reading and writing competencies determined by achievement scores or other standardized measures is that these scores and measures assume literacy is a cognitive ability. And yet, over the past four decades, researchers have argued that literacy is more than one's innate ability to read and write (Heath, 1983; Moje, 2000; Purcell-Gates, 2007; Purcell-Gates, Jacobson, & Degener, 2004). Print and other symbol systems are crucial to literacy practices, but we must recognize that the "learning and use of symbols is mediated by and constituted in social systems and cultural practices" (p. 109).

Reading and writing are embedded within social and cultural practices (Barton & Hamilton, 1998; Moje, 2000; Purcell-Gates, 2007; Purcell-Gates, Jacobson, & Degener, 2004), and "literacy is best considered an ideological construct as opposed to an autonomous skill, separable from contexts of use" (Purcell-Gates, 2007, p. 3). For example, David Kirkland's (2013) work provides in-depth examinations of language, race, and literacies. Therefore, we must look at people's reading and writing, the contexts where these practices occur, how they are used in everyday life, and their identities and ideologies. We cannot divorce the meanings people assign and attribute to their reading and writing from who they are.

Too often, when we refer to court-involved youths as illiterate or struggling readers and writers, we refer to how they decode print-based text on achievement or other standardized tests. We do not look at their reading via social media, writing poetry in journals, or finding solace in young adult literature. The stigma of being labeled a struggling reader and writer based on our assumption of what literacy is is damaging. A narrow view of literacy masks the complex ways court-involved youths engage in reading and writing. Furthermore, it dismisses the literacy practices that are important in their lives and perpetuates a sense of failure.

This also has implications for the ways we teach youths. Too often in educational settings, youths who are labeled struggling or reluctant readers and writers are assigned a skills-based curriculum intent on remediating their reading issues, further disengaging them because reading and writing are reinforced as skills—skills that they are lacking and skills that are separate from how they use reading and writing in their everyday lives. The dominant view of court-involved youths as illiterate, struggling readers and writers, compounded with the overall assumption of what it means to be "literate" and the type of education they need, contributes to their marginalization and the deficit view of their lives. This influences not only society's perception of youths but also the value and expectations we have for their lives.

A PRACTITIONER'S JOURNEY

As with any story, my path to working in this setting wasn't linear but filled with twists and turns as I navigated my professional life in education. Prior to my current work as a researcher and professor, I was a high school English teacher. The last high school that I taught in was a large, urban high school in the southwestern United States. The high school was considered "good," and according to many traditional measures, the school was successful. The faculty and staff were enthusiastic, and a high number of students passed the state achievement tests.

But at the time, there was an undercurrent of turmoil, and I was teaching students faced with enormous challenges. For example, conversations about immigration policies, which influenced where the school's students could attend, were heated. Inside school, students were faced with educational policies that dismissed their cultural capital and strengths. For example, there were many discussions in the teachers' lounge about whether it was acceptable for students to speak their native languages in class. An accepted reality for many schools in my district was a high dropout rate.

I began to realize not only that school was a place where some students felt they couldn't succeed but also that schools were organized to prevent some students from succeeding. As a teacher I felt that I was a firsthand witness to the school-to-prison pipeline. For the first time in my teaching career, I had students whose probation officers escorted them to class, and I overheard conversations between students about involvement in gang-related activity. I watched policies and circumstances contribute to students' failures in school. These experiences were unsettling and led to questions, not only about school policy, but also about the students in my classroom.

Juan was one such student. He entered my class every day, went directly to his desk, and slumped in the back. Despite my attempts, he never opened the class anthology and refused to complete any work. I didn't even consider Juan a reluctant student, but rather he was completely disengaged. His attendance was also problematic, as he was in and out of the alternative classroom for students with in-school suspensions.

One day, Juan took a quiz on *Romeo and Juliet* and received a 100%. I was surprised. I talked to him about his grade, and he shrugged and was dismissive of my interest. I started to look around and became increasingly aware of the students who attended my class with personal reading and writing materials in hand but seemed to struggle academically. I noticed students similar to Juan whose writing journals were filled with pages of ink but who never turned in a class writing assignment. I began to ask what was happening in my classroom and if our school was contributing to my students' struggles and disengagement. I wondered if we might be dismissing students who were very much active readers and writers by not drawing on their personal lives and instead focusing on what we perceived as deficits.

This teaching experience left me with unanswered questions that would later turn into the focus of my research career. After I left the district, I began spending time in the classroom of my friend Tom, who was teaching at Alexander Alternative School. His background was in math education; however, the alternative school asked him to teach all subject areas to students ranging from grades 4 to 12. I wanted to explore with him ways to facilitate reading and writing workshops in his classroom. The opportunity to work with him was really a chance encounter; however, it was a moment that propelled my career trajectory.

Tom and I were searching for stories to read with his students. With no money for new materials, he was at the mercy of various school districts to donate their books. One day we were flipping through worn and dated literature anthologies and lamenting the condition of the books. While looking at the publication date of a book, Tom stopped and told me to look at a name listed in the front cover of the textbook; it was the name of one of the probation officers. This anthology text was her book when she was in middle school. We were dismayed and sought grant funding to build a classroom library. What we discovered is that when students had access to books they wanted to read, they became avid readers, devouring anything from Suzanne Collins's *The Hunger Games* to Gareth Hinds's *Beowulf.*

As I spent more time in Tom's classroom, I had more and more conversations with students about what they liked to read and write when they were detained, while in school, and during their personal time. In my doctoral studies, I started reading more deeply from an interdisciplinary perspective about marginalized and disenfranchised youth. I read Delpit (1995/2006), Fine (1991), and Foucoult (1995). Maxine Greene's *Releasing the Imagination* (1995) resonated with me, as I, too, question society's perception of marginalized youth:

> Far too seldom are such young people looked upon as beings capable of imagining, of choosing, and of acting from their own vantage points on perceived possibility. Instead, they are subjected to outside pressures, manipulations, and predictions. The supporting structures that exist are not used to sustain a sense of agency among those they shelter; instead, they legitimate treatment, remediation, control—anything but difference and release. (p. 41)

And while educational researchers contributed to my thinking about youth in this setting, I was also motivated and inspired by people in mainstream settings working with marginalized populations. Father Gregory Boyle of Homeboy Industries (http://www.homeboyindustries.org) was integral in how I thought about my work, specifically his beliefs that everyone has an important story that deserves attention. He writes, "If there is a fundamental challenge within these stories, it is simply to change our lurking suspicion that some lives matter less than other lives" (2011, p. xiii). His work reinforced my ideas that marginalized youth, particularly those who have been detained or incarcerated, deserve to have their personal literacy practices validated; to be part of a community of writers; and to have teachers who encourage them to think, create, produce, ask questions, and write.

Reading the work of others who were working with marginalized populations wasn't enough. I decided to ask six girls, Molly, Suzanne, Danielle, Mia, Kelly, and Neveah, if I could study their reading and writing practices in a more in-depth manner. They were all Caucasian; their ages ranged from 13 to 17; and they had all occupied such spaces as detention centers, rehabilitation centers, and alternative schools, as well as their traditional middle and high schools.

Molly, Suzanne, and Neveah immediately and enthusiastically said yes because they identified themselves as writers and discussed writing poetry on a daily basis. Mia and Kelly agreed to participate but made it known that they didn't think they were "good" readers and writers, and they didn't like to write. And when I asked Danielle to participate, she responded, "Sure, but I hate reading and writing. I mean, I can do it, but I don't like it." Despite the range of the girls, I noticed the role of literacy in their lives, from the very intense claims that they had to write every day to the more nuanced role of reading materials, such as magazines, that they didn't consider "reading." I traveled with them through various spaces—and the more I learned about their lives out of school, the more I became bothered by their lives in school. I was especially troubled by Molly's situation.

Molly loved to write. She constantly was writing poems and journal entries. She found solace and comfort in writing, and she also shared her writing with family members as a way to communicate with them. During her sophomore year, she transitioned from a juvenile detention center to a drug rehabilitation center to a jail-based alternative school and then back to her traditional high school. Her English teacher recognized her academic potential, saying, "Molly is very bright academically. She's a lot smarter than what she likes everyone else to believe."

But although she felt Molly was capable of being placed in honors classes, she didn't feel comfortable placing Molly in a college preparatory course because she missed "weeks at a time" when she was placed in the alternative school or detention center (Pytash, 2016). As a teacher educator, I have returned to Molly's story many times—particularly the fact that her involvement in juvenile court kept her from entering advanced courses.

I've told this story to other teachers, and I have been alarmed by some of their responses. Most often teachers will say, "I don't teach *those* types of students." This response troubles me. And if you are reading this book and you also assume that this book is not about students you teach, I ask you to suspend those thoughts for a moment because the reality is that you might be teaching these students or you might unintentionally be harmfully labeling the students in your classroom. The challenge when reading this book is to question your assumptions about what it means to be a writer; the most effective ways to teach writers; and how we can best cultivate intellectually and civically engaged students by valuing their needs, voices, and potential.

My preservice teachers have firsthand knowledge of the problem of stereotyping which types of youth populate a detention center. My preservice teachers were involved in two field experiences: On Monday nights they facilitated a writing group with me at the local detention center, and their "Teaching Composition" course was embedded at a local suburban middle school, one that is primarily white, middle class, and considered an "excellent" school. Imagine their surprise when they showed up on Monday night and a student they had been working with from that middle school classroom was at the detention center. This reinforces the importance of remembering that "those" youths do not live in a vacuum. They navigate communities, detention centers, counseling facilities, and our middle and high schools.

CONCLUSION

This book offers examples, stories, and writings from my experiences. It chronicles my journey from someone who dropped into an experience in an alternative school to someone who sees this work as central to my current job as a teacher educator and literacy researcher.

As I position myself as the author of this book, I recognize that I have the unearned privilege of being a white female academic—one who enters and leaves the detention center at will—and my research and writing about youths in juvenile detention centers contributed to my career as a scholar and academic. My lived experiences have been significantly different than those of the youths featured in this book. I do not claim to have the same under-standings about their experiences within the juvenile justice system, but I do claim a great responsibility as I think about the ways youths are portrayed and represented. The youths featured in this book have trusted me with their life stories and their writings.

There are many things that this book does; however, there are also things that this book does not do. This book is not necessarily a critique of the juvenile justice system, although I do maintain a critical stance when exam-ining the educational opportunities for youths while detained, confined, and incarcerated. I would encourage readers to explore books that provide critical portraits of the juvenile justice system, such as *No Place for Children* (Liss, 2005), *No Matter How Loud I Shout* (Humes, 1996), and *Burning Down the House* (Bernstein, 2014).

In addition, this book is not a "silver bullet" that explains how engaging youths in writing will keep them out of detention centers, and it certainly is not supposed to represent all youths who have attended alternative schools and detention centers. The book is an intentional and critical examination of the complex role of literacy in the lives of court-involved young adults. The purpose of this book is to provide an in-depth look at how writing might possibly be the best opportunity to give students tools to deal with their circumstances: a voice to express themselves, an opportunity to recognize their strengths, a way to document their aspirations, and a chance at hope.

Furthermore, this book advocates for literacy instruction grounded in re-search and for youths to be creative meaning-makers. Finally, this book underscores the power of writing as a way to amplify beliefs and life experi-ences. I hope this book is evidence that these youths aren't throwaways; they are young adults, and their lives are filled with happiness, sadness, complexity, and turmoil. Despite what some think, they are authors, producers, and designers.

The remainder of this book is organized according to themes that have emerged from my work:

• Research on writing instruction in schools
• A framework for writing instruction
• Identity, trauma, and relationships
• Writing about social issues
• Using technology for composition

Each chapter begins with a piece of youth writing. This is purposeful and highlights the writing youths do in their lives and in classrooms. Throughout the chapters are sections titled "In Action," which feature particular young adults and their writing experiences. These stories provide implications for our writing instruction. Finally, featured in the chapters are "Instructional Principles," which focus on the design and implementation of writing instruction. These instructional principles are research-based and drawn from working closely with youth in juvenile detention centers.

* * *

Jimmy Santiago Baca, a poet and teacher who spent the majority of his adolescence in prison, stated that when he learned to read and write in prison, he realized his life was worth living. In his memoir, *A Place to Stand* (2002), he writes that learning to read and write while incarcerated taught him "to believe in (himself) and to dream for a better life" (p. 4). He states, "[L]iteracy is freedom and everyone has something significant to say" (2010, p. xiv). The youths featured in this book do have something significant to say, and this is an attempt to have their voices heard.

Chapter One

The Research on Writing Instruction

This chapter provides a general overview of the research on writing instruction in schools; examines the concerns and limitations of current pedagogical practices; and provides an overview of the process approach to writing, which serves as the foundation for the instructional approaches in this book. This chapter takes a broader look at underlying beliefs that shape our view of students as writers. Woven throughout the chapter are citations from current reports and policy statements. There are three main sections:

1. Research on Writing Instruction in Schools. This section presents current research on writing instruction in schools. These reports are important for writing teachers because they have implications for our instructional practices.

2. Concerns About This Trend. Educators need to have a critical lens when it comes to current educational trends. We need to be discerning and consider how instructional approaches promote youths as writers.

3. A Research-Based Foundation for Writing Instruction. It is important for educators to have a conceptual understanding of writing instruction in order to effectively implement pedagogical practices.

RESEARCH ON WRITING INSTRUCTION IN SCHOOLS

In 2002, the College Board established the National Commission on Writing in America's Schools and Colleges to examine effective writing pedagogy and provide instructional recommendations. The commission's *The Neglected "R"* contends that despite the importance of writing to students' success in school and in their future careers, writing instruction in schools had been largely ignored in the curriculum, or if it was taught, it was widely formulaic (College Entrance Examination Board, 2003). The commission

" "The New Faith."

a new beginning,
shot like bullets straight to the Son.
A new Journey has just begun.
A new thought behind every piece of life.
A new way to explain the things you dar
What lies beyond the reach of reality and a dr
The path you choose to walk,
         your
Everything that's meant to be.
Will eventually come if you just follow me.
a peculiar hand that reaches to the m
the fear of dying will be over soon.
The clock will tick like a bomb in
head.
Everything is easier left unsaid,
Beyond the Galaxy something impossible
see,
Seems in distance, from where I stand
Life is better directed by hand.
a unbelievable, but you see my God,
will direct you the way,
He'll find something new

Molly's poem "The New Faith"

argues for a "writing agenda," including increased writing time, an emphasis on using technology, development of effective assessments and measurements of writing, and additional professional development for teachers.

The report was hailed as groundbreaking and inspired professional organizations to respond in a variety of ways. For example, the National Writing Project cites the report as encouraging professional development in the teaching of writing, while the National Commission on Writing published follow-up reports with specific guidelines for extending writing time and instruction in schools (e.g., Newkirk & Kent, 2007).

Researchers continued to investigate writing pedagogy in schools. Applebee and Langer (2009, 2011) followed *The Neglected "R"* with a series of studies to explore writing instruction at a national level. Over a four-year period, they examined writing instruction broadly through national surveys and in-depth case studies. They also found that overall, students were not writing a significant amount, and students were particularly limited in the amount of extended writing they were asked to produce. Applebee and Langer (2011) report:

> Of the 8,542 separate assignments that we gathered from 138 case study students in these schools (a sampling of all of their written work in the four core content areas during a semester), only 19% represented extended writing of a paragraph or more; all the rest consisted of fill in the blank and short answer exercises, and copying of information directly from the teacher's presentation—types of activities that are best described as writing without composing. (Results were similar for middle school and high school students, with 20.9% and 17.6% of their work, respectively, involving extended writing.)

Applebee and Langer's (2011) report demonstrates that writing was not being used for students to demonstrate their thinking or new learning, nor was it being taught as a craft to communicate ideas, thoughts, and opinions through extensive and varied writing assignments. Many teachers blamed high-stakes testing for the emphasis on short response.

In addition, those teachers who did report or demonstrate extensive writing assignments were typically teaching in International Baccalaureate schools or advanced placement classrooms. This means that students at schools without these programs or not placed in these advanced classes were not receiving the same opportunities for writing instruction and writing. Rather, students considered academically "average" or "struggling" received minimal writing instruction, predominantly focused on test preparation.

What this research points out is that all too often time to write is relegated to prescriptive exercises or timed writing for practice on standardized tests. For example, teachers begin class with 5 to 10 minutes devoted to students completing a worksheet that is submitted to the teacher, who then marks the worksheet for correct responses. Or once a week, students receive a lined piece of paper, are given a prompt, and are asked to write at least 25 lines about the subject within the given time.

While this might be an assessment of writing, neither of these scenarios are time in which students receive writing instruction. Nor are the students in these scenarios truly engaged in the act of writing. Instead, writing is condensed to an assessment of knowledge or an assessment of prescriptive skills that we assume are necessary for certain grade levels. Unfortunately, this type of writing is not conducive to (1) developing students as writers; (2) helping adolescents view themselves as writers; and (3) conveying that writing is a worthwhile pursuit. Furthermore, as research highlights, classrooms that do provide effective and research-based writing instruction tend to be limited to advanced courses or specialized schools. Therefore, those without access to specialized programs or classes are most likely receive minimal effective writing instruction—if any instruction at all. This perpetuates a certain privilege for the already academically successful students and increases the gap in students' rhetorical knowledge.

IN ACTION: MOLLY

Reading literature aloud and answering questions on a worksheet or completing grammar worksheets is typical in Mrs. Phillips's 10th-grade English language arts class. She explains, "They do a lot of answering questions. They define vocabulary words. That is something that is an ongoing thing. I constantly have them do that. There are not too many essay questions. We don't do too many of those, but we do short answers. You know, maybe four or five sentences for each answer. That's mostly what we do." She later explains that "hard writing" is reserved for later in the sophomore year.

Molly, whose work is featured at the beginning of this chapter and who is described in the introduction of this book, is one of Mrs. Phillips's students. Molly writes poetry every day in a notebook full of her poems. She declares that she writes poetry because of people and how they make her feel. She also writes poetry to get her "emotions off her chest." Despite this, she explains, "it is funny because I love writing, but I hate English class." But Molly also says that she "definitely" would like English class "if we could write poetry."

Mrs. Phillips knows Molly is an avid writer and yet doesn't try to engage her in English class through writing. Even worse, she deliberately holds her back from taking advanced courses, despite thinking Molly could academically do the work, because of her involvement in the juvenile court system.

CONCERNS ABOUT THIS TREND

The fact that students do not receive adequate writing instruction in school cannot be ignored. It is particularly troublesome because writing is a necessary skill for academic achievement and workplace success. The emphasis of writing only on standardized tests is harmful because students see writing only as a skill only to be assessed. Having students write for test preparation negates the importance of writing and overlooks important factors about writing and writing instruction:

1. Students' writing dispositions are crucial for developing their identities as writers.
2. Writing has authentic purposes and audiences.

Students' Writing Dispositions

When students walk into our writing classrooms, they carry with them their perceptions of themselves as writers, often determined by their impressions of past writing experiences; for example, the feedback they have received on their writing in the past or grades they have received on writing assignments. Past successes or failures often influence what they choose to do or to avoid.

Researchers have found that students' beliefs about their writing abilities are a predictor of their performance on writing tasks (Pajares 2003; Pajares, Johnson, & Usher, 2007). This means students' beliefs about themselves as writers influence what they actually do. For example, if students think of themselves as capable, then they are more likely to be fully engaged in the writing task. Therefore, students' writing identities—how they view themselves as writers—are crucial to our classrooms.

Scholars who have investigated students' dispositions toward writing have identified three main constructs: confidence, perseverance, and passion (Piazza & Siebert, 2008). Therefore, our goals as teachers are to:

1. Help students gain confidence in their writing. Closely related to self-efficacy, student confidence "reflects faith or belief in an individual's ability to write and a certainty about his or her effectiveness as a writer" (Piazza & Siebert, 2008, p. 278). Teachers can help students gain confidence by implementing practices that provide students choice in writing topics, opportunities to confer and talk about writing, and extended writing time.
2. Support students as they learn how to persevere through the difficulties of writing. Persistence during writing tasks refers to student's "willingness to spend time writing and expend effort" on their writing (Piazza & Siebert, 2008, p. 278). As teachers, we need to teach stu-

dents strategies to help them learn how to persist through the difficult times of writing.

3. Encourage students to be passionate writers. Students who choose to write voluntarily or who have a desire to write can be considered passionate writers. As teachers, we need to create moments so our students can find joy in writing.

As writing teachers, we must create positive experiences that foster confidence, persistence, and passion, so students can then begin to see themselves as writers and writing as an avenue for voicing their experiences, beliefs, and opinions.

Writing Has a Purpose and Audience

Educators who work with youths often believe that students who lack "foundational skills" for writing need instruction that emphasizes how to grammatically construct a sentence or use proper punctuation. While students need instruction that focuses on grammar and syntax, if this is the only instruction they receive, then the educators are missing crucial elements in teaching writing. Writing is relegated to a short response or a memorized acronym for composing a short answer to an exam question. This neglects students' needs to understand why people write, who the audience is, and how language is used to communicate.

In 2016, the National Council of Teachers of English (NCTE) published a position statement about the knowledge that educators need to teach writing. While the statement includes 10 main issues related to writing (e.g., writing related to talk, fair and authentic assessments, the writing process, and the relationship between reading and writing), the policy report specifically states that teachers who have professional knowledge of writing will acknowledge that "writing grows out of many purposes."

Writing with a purpose helps students write with specific goals in mind; for example, to develop an argument, to tell a story, or to convey information. When students know why they are writing, the writing task becomes more relevant and meaningful. In addition, students can begin to recognize the intended audience of their writing. Flower (1979) explains this cognitive process by using the terms *writer-based prose* versus *reader-based prose*. Writer-based prose occurs when students write as if they are the reader of the piece instead of conceptualizing how others might read their writing. Novice writers often write from this stance as they are trying to articulate their thoughts and ideas. However, when writers know the purpose and intended audience for their writing, then they can write reader-based prose, which means they are considering how an audience might interpret their writing.

When students have metaknowledge or knowledge of purpose and audience, they are able to clearly articulate their thoughts and ideas.

When students have a sense of the writing purpose and audience, they can begin to think critically about using language to communicate their ideas. In this instance teachers can embed instruction that focuses on using appropriate syntax and language. For example, when teaching argumentative writing, teachers can include lessons about sentence variety. Students who need explicit instruction in complex sentences can benefit from a teacher pointing out how the sentence structure influences the way an audience reads a piece. When writing poetry, teachers can discuss how authors can intentionally break grammar "rules," similar to the ways e. e. cummings does not use capitalization or Emily Dickinson uses hyphens. The focus on syntax is contextualized within a larger focus on purpose and audience. Students then begin to recognize how authors are strategic and intentional in their writing decisions.

Teachers can also provide lessons on the ways language is a social and cultural construct. NCTE's (2016) position statement reminds teachers of the importance of having conversations with students about how "cultural differences are not only linguistic but also racial, economic, geographic, and ideological."

Our goal is to teach students how to use language flexibly so they can write for a variety of purposes and audiences (NCTE, 2016). Nevertheless, we must be careful not to purposefully ignore, overlook, or criticize our students' languages. Delpit (2008) contends that damage occurs when teachers work to erase a person's language because "language is one of the most intimate expressions of identity, indeed, 'the skin we speak,'" so "to reject a person's language can only feel as if we are rejecting him" (p. 47). Ignoring and pushing aside students' languages is detrimental to their views of themselves as writers as well as their understanding of purpose, audience, and using language to communicate ideas. Ultimately, our attitude is what narrows a student's opinion of what counts as writing and who counts as a writer.

A RESEARCH-BASED FOUNDATION FOR WRITING INSTRUCTION

A surge of writing research occurred in the 1970s and 1980s. Writing scholars, such as Emig (1977), Flower and Hayes (1981), and Shaughnessy (1976), investigated students' thinking and process when writing. Scholars began to document the complexity of writing—acknowledging that writers must have knowledge of what they want to say, how to effectively state their ideas, the writing process, and strategies to help them during the process.

While writers might move through various stages of writing (prewriting, drafting, revising), it became apparent that writing is not a linear, lockstep approach but rather a dynamic and recursive process in which writers are consistently returning to their goals, drafting ideas, and revising their pieces.

This seminal knowledge about the composition process led to new ideas about how to teach writing. Writing scholars Nancie Atwell, Lucy Calkins, Donald Graves, and Donald Murray pioneered writing workshops built on the idea that writing is a process. This model of instruction emphasizes that students need ample time to write, to confer about their writing, and to revise based on feedback. The emphasis is not necessarily on the final product but rather on the process of writing.

Today educators endorse the power of writing workshops in classrooms from kindergarten (Ray, 2006) through high school (Gallagher, 2011; Kittle, 2008). Researchers continue to investigate writing taught as a process, and Graham and Perin's *Writing Next* (2007), a meta-analysis of empirical research, identifies 11 elements of instructional approaches beneficial for student writers. The overall effect of implementing strategies aligned with a process approach was significant and included a number of activities, such as

> creating extended opportunities for writing; emphasizing writing for real audiences; encouraging cycles of planning, translating, and reviewing; stressing personal responsibility and ownership of writing projects; facilitating high levels of student interactions; developing supportive writing environments; encouraging self-reflection and evaluation; and offering personalized individual assistance, brief instructional lessons to meet students' individual needs, and, in some instances, more extended and systematic instruction. (p. 19)

The process approach to writing, specifically within a writing workshop model, allows for writers to see their writing develop over time and truly engage in the act of writing a piece through multiple drafts. In addition, writing workshops are based on the idea that writing is not a solo endeavor; rather writers are members of communities who can talk about the craft of writing.

Despite this research documenting how people write and best practices when teaching writing, writing is largely ignored in the curriculum or is taught in a prescriptive manner.

CONCLUSION

This chapter provides an overview of the research documenting the dismal ways writing is taught in schools. Even worse is that our instruction marginalizes students by not teaching writing because they are not in certain courses or attending certain schools. Though teachers certainly feel the pressure of standardized testing, we need to remember that we cannot teach students to write unless we let them write. Teaching students how to write is more than simply fixing grammar in sentences or evaluating how much students can write within a given time period. If we want students to grow as writers, we need to talk to them about their writing, and then we need to let them write more. A prescriptive, skills-based approach to writing not only oversimplifies the writing process but also creates a narrow definition of writing that limits our students' growth as writers who can craft intentional pieces.

The underlying assumption of the cited policy statements and research is that, with effective instruction, all young adults can continue to grow and develop as writers. This requires us to incorporate research-based writing instruction that honors students' identities as writers and their languages while teaching them how to craft writing for specific purposes and audiences. The types of writing we ask of students must be intricately tied to the adolescents in our classroom, so that they are central to the instructional approaches we adopt. This provides us insights into their dispositions as writers, the connection between their identities, and the many ways they take up and engage in writing.

Chapter Two

Reading Like a Writer

I went to jail over nothing.

I was walking down my street when my mom's boyfriend was driving. He swerved and tried to hit me with his white van with bars on the windows. He jumped out of the van, grabbed me, and tried to hit me—swinging on me. Before he knew what was coming, I punched him in the mouth, and his jaw rattled like pennies in a coffee can.

He went to his van, got on his phone, and called the cops. Ten or fifteen minutes later, the cops pulled up and ask what happened. He told them his story, and then I told them mine. Of course they believed his story, and he pressed domestic charges. Ten minutes after they cuffed me, it was the slammer for me. Now I'm locked up, and they won't tell me how long I'm going to be here for.

The police always believe the adults instead of the child. It's because in their eyes they think the adult is always right. They think adults never lie—but that's the damn lie—adults always lie. The police should have put him in here and not me.

I went to jail over nothing.

* * *

While the process approach provides a broad framework for teaching writing, there are multiple ways to structure writing pedagogy to develop students as writers. One way to frame instruction within the writing workshop model is to teach students to *read like writers* (Smith, 1983). Students learn to *read like writers* when they have the opportunity to study how a particular piece of writing or a genre is crafted. Together, teachers and students read and analyze exemplar or model texts. Students' attention is directed to how authors write and the intentional decisions they make while writing. This knowledge, in turn, is used to guide students during their own writing.

Scholars and practitioners use the term *units of study* when multiple pieces of the same genre are read, studied, and analyzed by students (Ray, 2006). Instead of closely studying just one piece, students have the opportunity to explore in depth a particular genre through multiple pieces. This inquiry approach scaffolds students as they learn how the genre is crafted, its purpose, and its audience.

This instructional approach is supported by research. In *Writing Next* (2007) Graham and Perin reference studies on the positive effect of that exemplary models had on students' growth as writers. And a current report published by the Institute of Education Sciences (Graham et al., 2016) finds that students who study exemplar or model texts during writing instruction develop metaknowledge and knowledge of domains text features and procedures:

1. *Metaknowledge.* Students learn the purpose of the piece of writing. If students can identify the purpose for writing (e.g., to establish an argument or to tell a story) and recognize the intended reader, then they can write with specific goals in mind, which Graham and Perin (2007) note has a positive effect on students' writing quality. When students are encouraged to ask questions about why and how authors compose, they are engaged in conversations about audience. A goal of our instruction is to help students recognize that authors craft with a specific purpose and an audience in mind. Students who understand how and why authors write are more likely to be engaged and motivated as writers.

2. *Domains.* Students learn content. When students read mentor texts to study writing, they are also engaged in the close reading and rereading of texts. This allows them to critically process and comprehend their reading. Writing also helps students to think through complex ideas and articulate their understanding of specific content.

3. *Text Features.* Students learn textual characterization related to particular genres. One of the goals of using mentor texts or units of study is to help students recognize features of genres. Students read multiple pieces to understand a genre's organizational structure and appropriate discourse. Students then recognize patterns across pieces of texts, including their own piece of writing, which helps them to consider what is effective writing and how they might incorporate specific elements into their own work.

4. *Procedures.* Students learn more about the writing process and strategies. Students need opportunities to reflect on their writing process. Some students might like to free write as a brainstorming exercise,

while others might want to use a visual organizer to plan their writing. Because students are focused on the craft of writing rather than a final product, they have the opportunity to focus on the process and strategies that can support their process. This learning occurs because students are not just replicating a certain mentor or model text but rather are thinking critically about how genres are constructed (Ray, 2006). This is why we must refocus our efforts on implementing writing workshops in all classrooms. This cannot be reserved for "good" writers; all writers benefit from this instruction because the basics are embedded in a larger examination of writing.

As writing teachers, we do not need to compromise our beliefs about instruction because of where we teach or who our students are. Rather, we should implement writing instruction that is grounded in years of writing pedagogy research.

INSTRUCTIONAL PRINCIPLES

Our goal for students is to develop their metaknowledge, content knowledge, text feature knowledge, and procedural knowledge. The "Reading Like a Writer" framework can guide our instruction in juvenile detention facilities with these four design principles:

1. Adapting Instruction. Lack of time is a concern in any classroom, and this is certainly true in juvenile detention facilities; however, teachers can strategically integrate the "Reading Like a Writer" approach into their classrooms.

2. Uncovering Structure. Teachers must highlight how genres follow a particular structure.

3. Learning the Discourse. Teachers must invite students to use the discourse of writers.

4. Talking About Writing. Teachers and students must engage in conversations about writing as they confer about student work.

ADAPTING INSTRUCTION

Supported by years of research in traditional schools, writing workshops, particularly the "Reading Like a Writer" approach, seems difficult at first to implement in a detention center because of the unique factors that influence these educational experiences.

First, detention centers are transient in nature. They tend to be short-term placements for youths, typically between two and four weeks in pre-adjudication and postadjudication facilities. There are times, however, when an adolescent is arrested, detained, and released in just a 24-hour period. Or the opposite occurs, and depending on trial and sentencing, an adolescent can spend months in juvenile detention. This means that youth are constantly coming and leaving without teachers knowing for certain how long their students will be in class. This transience is a major factor in how instruction can be implemented.

Second, youths come to detention centers with varying educational experiences, knowledge, and abilities. Youths are often assigned to a pod or group that they live with during their time in detention. Typically, they are placed in groups based on age; however, this grouping can also be related to their charges or sentences. Students attend class with their pods; therefore, one class can have students who span grade levels, background knowledge, and prior writing experiences. In some sense, writing instruction must be "one-size fits all" and at the same time differentiated to meet all students' needs. Therefore, teachers are challenged to conceptualize instruction that can work with students of differing levels and varying background knowledge.

To adapt instruction, teachers must be aware of the broader conceptual goals of instruction. Writing is a craft, and students need opportunities to learn writing strategies. Once these goals are acknowledged, teachers can implement specific pedagogical approaches. The teacher must break down instruction into steps that build on one another to support the entire framework for students' learning. In this way, instruction is adapted to fit each unique classroom.

"Reading Like a Writer" can be adapted for a juvenile detention center classroom to meet students' specific needs. Introducing exemplary pieces of writing and constantly teaching students how to read closely helps all students to grow as writers, even with various experiences.

IN ACTION: AMANDA'S WRITING WORKSHOPS

Amanda, a teacher at a local detention center, wanted to implement writing workshops. The detention center where she taught was considered a short-term facility; students typically were at the facility for two weeks at a time. This significantly shaped Amanda's instructional goals, as she always had to consider who would be new to her classroom and who would be leaving her classroom. In addition, Amanda also recognized that most of her students returned to their traditional home schools after being in the detention center, and so she understood the importance of their academic engagement. Based on the "Reading Like a Writer" framework, she developed weekly instructional plans.

In traditional schools units of study can span multiple weeks, but the transient nature of Amanda's classroom dictated that instruction occurred over the course of a week. The goal was to provide instruction that was short but intense. She believed that one week would provide enough time for students to analytically read exemplar texts and write an original piece. The basic framework she developed was used each week, regardless of genre.

Day 1

1. Use two to three quality pieces as models to represent how the student piece will be written.
2. Pick one model. Using a transparency, show students how to deconstruct the text. Read through and highlight the intentional decisions the author made. For example, in memoirs and persuasive pieces, the author uses *I*.
3. List the observed features on the board.
4. Have students independently or in pairs find the same features in the second model.
5. Go through the model with the students. Explicitly point out the features in the text. Remind students that when they write, they will be using these features in their own writing.
6. Allow students time to brainstorm writing ideas.

Day 2

1. Review the features from the day before.
2. Allow students the whole class period to write their rough drafts.
3. Walk around the classroom, conferring with students about their pieces of writing and their ideas.
4. Collect drafts. Read, and add one or two questions or positive comments to spark additional writing for the next day.

Day 3

1. Read model text aloud. Point out one thing for students to focus on. For example, if students are reading and writing memoirs, point out how the author uses descriptions and details. Or if teaching articles, have students pay attention to the author's opening and ending sentences.
2. Hand back student drafts.
3. Have students look at their rough drafts to look for the feature you pointed out. Have them try out these ideas in their writing.
4. Provide students time to revise their work.

Day 4

Note: This day follows the same format as day 3. This is purposeful and allows for the teacher to select another part of student writing to focus on. This may be a literary element, such as figurative language, or a grammar lesson, such as writing more complex sentences.

1. Read model text aloud, pointing out one thing for students to focus on.
2. Hand back student drafts.
3. Have students look at their rough drafts for the feature you pointed out. Have them try out these ideas in their writing.
4. Provide students time to revise their work.

Day 5

1. Have students write their final drafts.
2. Decide if it is appropriate for students to share their writing aloud or in small groups.

The first time Amanda implemented a writing workshop based on the "Reading Like a Writer" approach, she focused on teaching memoirs. Amanda started with this genre because she felt most comfortable as a teacher talking to students about memoirs and thought the narrative storytelling would appeal to many young adults.

The week began by selecting four to five quality pieces to serve as models. Amanda selected three texts from the anthology *Guys Write for Guys Read* (Scieszka, 2008a), including "Anything Can Happen" (Oppel, 2008), "Brothers" (Scieszka, 2008b), and "My Entire Football Career" (Bauer, 2008). In addition, she included a memoir published by Jerry O'Connell about his tryout to be a professional lifeguard (O'Connell, 2007).

On the first day, Amanda read aloud "Anything Can Happen" while thinking aloud and naming her observed features about the piece. For example, she discussed how the memoir focuses on an important moment in the author's life and how the author uses first person. Next, Amanda selected the memoir "My Entire Football Career." After reading the piece with students, the class discussed what they noticed. Amanda wrote all of their ideas on a piece of chart paper. Finally, students independently read the memoir "Brothers" and contributed their observed features to the chart paper.

After students had an opportunity to read memoirs, Amanda engaged the class in conversations about the purpose and audience of memoirs. Amanda referred back to the list of features posted on the wall and asked students to brainstorm why someone would write a memoir and why someone would read a memoir. Students shared their ideas, and Amanda transcribed them on an additional chart paper, which she hung on the wall to serve as a visual reminder for students.

Students then brainstormed important moments from their lives that they might want to write about, questions Amanda provided, such as

- Think about a time you laughed harder than ever before.
- Think about a time you did something good for someone else.
- What is something you will never forget?
- When were you 100% happy?
- What memory shows something important about your family or friends?

Throughout the week, Amanda first began the writing workshop by reading aloud a memoir and reviewing the class list of observed features. For example, when she noticed that there were a significant number of new students, she read Jerry O'Connell's (2007) piece to remind students that memoirs are used to share an important life event. This was a purposeful decision; if anyone was new to the class, then they were able to learn about the genre and important elements. The rest of the class period was designed for students to have time to write. During this time, Amanda circulated in the classroom to have individual conversations with students about their writing. This allowed her to help students who were new to the class and to continue to scaffold students who were in the process of writing.

Conferring with her students allowed her to notice that many students were struggling with their opening sentences. She decided to frame her reading and features instruction differently. This time, she read "Why Books Are Dangerous (Gaiman, 2008). Instead of generally calling attention to elements of memoirs, she specifically discussed how the author crafted the beginning and ending sentences. Amanda did a think-aloud so students would notice that the author begins and ends his piece with the same sentence, "Reading can be a dangerous thing." She then discussed how in the beginning of the piece, this seems like a ridiculous statement; however, after reading everything that happened to the author while he was reading, the statement makes sense. Her students then played with this idea and tried to tie their beginning and closing sentences together.

For example, one student, Patrick, was writing his memoir about an experience with his best friend. He began and ended his piece with "It was a dark and snowy night when I stole my first car." He explained that he used this opening to "catch the reader's attention," but the meaning behind the memoir focuses on the relationship with his best friend because they have "been through everything together."

Amanda then decided to spend the remainder of her time with students looking at how authors use rich language to describe an important life moment or event. In addition, Amanda taught students simile and metaphor and highlighted instances in the text where the authors used these literary devices. For example, another student, Evan, wrote about punching his mother's boyfriend in the mouth during a fistfight and how "his jaw rattled like pennies in a coffee can."

Engaging students in "Reading Like a Writer" explicitly highlights the connections between reading and writing, while emphasizing the important elements in crafting writing. Patrick demonstrated this when he explained, "Studying the other pieces first shows us what it is, like how to write one yourself. We studied description and starting and ending. We talked about using dialogue. When we compared all the memoirs, then I could think how I could, like, put those things in mine."

UNCOVERING STRUCTURE

As Amanda's vignette highlights, to support students' reading like writers, teachers can engage students using gradual release based on modeling, guided practice, and independent practice. The first two steps tend to be teacher-led:

1. After a genre of study is selected, teachers find exemplar pieces of the genre.
2. Thinking aloud, the teacher models how to deconstruct a text. Reading a piece of writing aloud, the teacher stops periodically to call students' attention to important elements of the genre.

The goal of this process is not for the teacher to be viewed as the expert but to demonstrate to students how to ask questions about the ways texts are written. Most students have not had opportunities to analyze texts in this manner, so they need teacher guidance to show them what they are expected to do. This positions students as active agents who possess knowledge and understanding about how to ask questions about the texts they encounter every day.

Because we want students to understand that writers write with purpose, we need to explicitly call their attention to the genres' broader purposes and audiences. Teachers can frame conversations around such questions as

• How can we describe this genre? Why would people read this?
• Who is the author? What might the author's intentions be for writing this piece?
• What is the purpose of this genre? What is the purpose of this specific piece of writing?

While teachers can certainly facilitate this conversation, this shouldn't be completely teacher-led. Asking students "What did you notice when reading that makes you think this?" invites students to go back to the writing and look for patterns.

This conversation also broadens students' ideas about genre. Typically, genres are treated as silos of narrative, informative, persuasive, and argumentative writing. In reality, genres are more nuanced. For example, persuasive feature articles typically start with a narrative vignette to hook a reader while also including evidence to support claims. Tweets can be classified as informative, descriptive, persuasive, or narrative, depending on the content. This process helps students to connect writing with their everyday lives, for example, when they search for YouTube videos, read blogs, scan magazine articles, or read poetry.

Students begin thinking about the choices that authors make when writing. They learn what a genre is and why people write in particular ways. In considering the broader purposes for a genre, we can focus students to look at the way an author has crafted a piece.

The structure of a piece of writing is the invisible framework or skeleton. It's how the author purposefully constructs the text. Understanding how a genre or piece is structured helps students to learn how authors convey their ideas.

There are many ways writing is structured; for example, memoirs tend to be chronological, and how-to books are sequential. In the vignette about Amanda, she purposefully directed students to notice that the author begins and ends his piece with the same line, "Reading can be a dangerous thing." She wanted students to recognize that this was intentional when the author structured his memoir.

In addition, teachers can look closer at syntax and how an author constructs sentences. Students need to learn how sentence structure controls the pace of writing and can draw a reader's attention to a particular point or suspenseful moment.

Directing students' attention to structure helps them to see that writing is intentional. Studying writing provides students with concrete ideas that they can borrow for their own writing. Another benefit is that students feel prepared to write and see that writing is not an insurmountable task but something they can accomplish. This process can build their confidence in writing.

IN ACTION: FOCUSED ON UNDERSTANDING THE MEANING
OF GENRE

Jamia, a 15-year-old black girl, was one of the students in Amanda's class during the memoir unit. She explained that reading the memoirs helped her "get ideas and see what it's supposed to be like." Jamia decided to write her memoir about an experience her little sister had with a bully. Jamia wrote that her sister Brianna, who was six, was being picked on by a little boy in her class. In order to defend herself, Brianna hit the boy and received three days of in-school suspension. Obviously, this memory was important to Jamia, but in the first draft, it was unclear why it was significant to her. After reading Jerry O'Connell's (2007) piece, Jamia highlighted the last two paragraphs of the memoir, noting that in those paragraphs he clearly states "what the event taught him and why it is important in his life."

Jamia went back to her original draft and made notes of where she could include details about the event. She noted that in the final paragraph, she should write about why the event was important to her and included the following sentence in her final draft: "I personally think I am a good sister for caring and explaining to Brianna that you can't hit people. I told her that and that I love her. Usually I would defend her, but that wouldn't be setting a good example because two wrongs don't make a right."

Through multiple readings of memoirs, Jamia recognized that she needed to write a memoir focused on an important life moment, and yet, she focused on an event that happened to her sister. Closely studying memoirs reinforced for Jamia that she needed to explicitly state the significance of this moment in her life. Interestingly, this moment was important because of what she did not do. Even though she loved her younger sister and wanted to defend her, she chose not to do so because she wanted to be a good example for her sister. This moment exemplified how Jamia viewed herself as a role model for her sister.

LEARNING THE DISCOURSE

Talking Like a Writer

Within the writing workshop, students are intentionally positioned as writers with the goal of taking ownership of their own writing. Writers make intentional decisions about their topics, how to best convey a message, and how to craft language.

Writers use the language of writers. Communities have a common language or discourse (Gee, 2004); therefore, students should know and use the language of writers—how writers talk about their craft. For example, some students may not be familiar with the word *genre* or the language used to classify genres. Acquiring the language of writers is important so students can talk about the decisions they make as writers. When we introduce students to writing, we peel back the layers of and teach them the language of the craft and how to be reflective when writing.

Learning How to Craft and Use Language While Writing

When students have opportunities to develop their voices as writers, they learn to recognize how authors use language to convey information, describe moments, or indicate bias. By analyzing the ways authors use language, students become familiar with new vocabulary, jargon, or patterns of speech. This also allows them to play with language and view language as a creative endeavor.

Students need opportunities to creatively consider word choice and the importance of individual words. This is a more granular aspect that teachers tend to teach in isolation as a discrete skill. For example, teachers may just point students toward a thesaurus to locate synonyms. Instead, we should teach students to analyze language and the ways it contributes to the overall goals of the piece. Reading and analyzing language in mentor texts serves as a guide for students and teachers to talk about the importance of words. Similarly, students should learn when and how to use literary devices to enhance their writing and to develop voice or their individual writing style.

Emphasizing word choice focuses students' attention on the ways authors intentionally use language. Teachers can use minilessons that focus on a specific, concrete aspect of writing. Though one aspect of writing is emphasized, it is taught under the umbrella of authors writing for a specific purpose and audience and takes on meaning. Language construction is contextualized, which develops student voice.

IN ACTION: LIKE PENNIES IN A COFFEE CAN

Evan was scrawny, with shaggy brown hair that often fell over his eyes. He was only in the eighth grade, and yet this was his third experience in the detention center. In class, he was polite and tried to actively participate in instruction. But underneath this polite demeanor, it was obvious that he was angry about something. His memoir revealed why anger was building inside him. He wrote about a fight with his mom's boyfriend, who ended up calling the cops on him. He explained, "It's one of the times I went to jail. I felt like it was unfair, and I just wanted to write about it. Like I wrote, the police always believe adults and not kids."

During class Evan used an author's strategies in his own writing. For example, when Evan shared the changes he made from his first draft to his final draft, he stated that he was most proud of the sentence "I punched him in the mouth, and his jaw rattled like pennies in a coffee can."

He explained that he first just wrote "so I punched him in the mouth"; "But then I started to think more about how it felt, and it felt like his jaw rattled. Later when we were reading 'Brothers' and Ms. Amanda was talking about figurative language, I decided to add, 'like pennies in a coffee can.'"

Evan also made the decision to start and end his memoir with the sentence "I went to jail over nothing." This was similar to the memoir "Reading Is Dangerous," which begins and ends with the same sentence. It was in this borrowing of structure that Evan could explicitly state his feelings of injustice.

"Reading Like a Writer" was a new process for Evan. He explained that reading the memoirs first was helpful when he was preparing to write and that the experience was different than what he usually does. He shared,

> I always go blank when I write. But the reading gave me some ideas and I liked them. Usually when teachers teach writing, they just talk about pronouns, adverbs, all stuff like that, like capitalization, grammar stuff. But that doesn't help me know how to write. But this time I put actual thought into it, and I actually studied words and what I should use. I thought about the words before I wrote them down. I thought before I wrote.

TALKING ABOUT WRITING

A crucial component during the writing workshop is talking to students about their writing, which helps them to develop writing goals, provides feedback on their writing, and boosts their self-confidence. Students at the detention center often share that they've never really had a teacher talk about their writing. In a conversation with Patrick and Evan, they discussed how teachers had typically given them feedback on their writing:

> Patrick: No one has ever complimented me on my writing, so I don't think I've ever really had confidence.

> Evan: Teachers don't do that. They don't tell you what you did good. They might just tell you "good job." But if you really do a good job, you want someone to actually point it out and explain why it's good and how you did.

When we position students as authors, we reposition ourselves from evaluators to members of the writing community. Atwell (1998) describes being a teacher in a writing workshop as an "*exhilarating* balance that allows me to function in my classroom as a listener *and* a teller, an observer *and* an actor, a collaborator *and* a critic *and* a cheerleader" (p. 21).

Kelly Gallagher (2006) describes the role of a writing teacher as similar to a coach providing feedback during the writing process. A coach continuously assesses an athlete and provides feedback and guidance to further develop the athlete's abilities. In addition, a coach supports an athlete's goals and provides encouragement to keep the athlete motivated. Therefore, writing teachers can more effectively guide students' writing development by moving from an evaluator of student's writing performance to a coach guiding, supporting, and encouraging student writers.

One way to coach students through writing is by talking to them about their writing during conferences. Writing conferences can happen at the beginning of the writing process to establish writing goals and needs. They can also be conversations that take place while students are drafting. It is important to note that there might not always be substantial time for conferences, particularly in detention centers; however, conferences do not have to be lengthy conversations. Conferring with students can be a quick and effective. For example, a teacher may ask

- What are your goals for this piece?
- Where is one paragraph that you are struggling with or one place in your writing where you feel stuck?
- Read a paragraph or sentence that you really like. What do you like about it? What do you think you did well?

The answers to any of these questions can be good indicators of where the student is in the writing process. We learn about students' decisions as writers when we have conversations with them during the process. We can also learn more about a student's decision making when we provide opportunities for reflection after writing.

It is important—particularly when working with writers who have not always had positive learning experiences—that we start with a positive feature of students' writing. We want to tell students what they did well, not only to boost their confidence, but also so they can see what they have learned and what they might be able to do in the future. In addition, we should take care with constructive feedback that our comments point to doable revisions. Again, particularly at a detention center when students do not have significant time to write, giving them a list of revisions is overwhelming. We want our feedback to help students focus on one or two items that they can work on.

After students have finished a piece of writing, they can create a "director's cut." Just like directors of movies release versions with their original approved edits, a director's cut gives writers the chance to talk about their decisions. Students can create their "director's cuts" in a number of ways. Students can use the comment feature in Word documents on their pieces.

They can also create a podcast or vlog on their stylistic choices and intentions while writing. As teachers, this provides insight into students' thinking about the writing process. For students, this provides the opportunity to be metacognitive and metareflective about their choices, which is how they develop as writers.

Engaging students in writing workshops allows teachers to look holistically at writing instruction, not just at a final product. When we look at their writing process and have conversations about their decision making and their strengths, then we have a better sense of their writing experience.

IN ACTION: AMANDA AND SHELBY'S CONFERENCE

Amanda sat down at the desk next to Shelby and asked, "What is the most important thing you want your reader to know about you after they read your memoir?" Shelby quickly responded, "I want people reading my memoir to know I am funny and smart and that the most important thing that ever happened to me was the day my little brother was born." Amanda nodded to acknowledge that she was listening to Shelby.

Knowing that many students who enter her classroom do not consider themselves "good" writers, Amanda began by praising Shelby for how she chronicled the events of her brother's birth: "You did a nice job explaining everything that happened—like when you entered the hospital room and saw your mom and also when you held your mom's hand until your brother was born." Shelby slowly smiled, pleased by the feedback.

Amanda knew that Shelby needed specific feedback, guidance, and direction in order to move forward with her draft, but she also did not want to overwhelm Shelby. She instructed Shelby to add more description: "You write, 'I got to my mom's room, and she looked like she was in a lot of pain.' How did you know this?" Shelby responded, "Her face was really red, and she was holding her stomach." Amanda explained that these details were what she meant when she told the class to "show," not just "tell," readers what was happening. Shelby nodded and wrote this note on her draft. Amanda ended the conference with one more piece of advice: "In the other memoirs we read in class, many authors explain the importance at the end of the memoir. Maybe you can think about how to do this as well." Nodding, Shelby wrote, "tell importance" at the end of her draft.

When Shelby submitted her final draft at the end of the week, she considered Amanda's feedback and added details, including how her mom looked when she entered the delivery room. She described her brother as having "blond hair and blue eyes, weighing 6.8 pounds." Shelby decided to end her memoir with "My brother cried a lot, but when he saw me, he stopped crying. That made me feel special and made me realize I was a big sister. That special day made me realize I was special and that I'll always put my family first."

CONCLUSION

When Amanda first introduced her class to memoirs, many students were unsure of the definitions of *genre* and *memoir*. Only providing students dictionary definitions would not have adequately prepared them to write original pieces. It was crucial that these new words were contextualized in readings of memoirs so students could truly grasp the literature to create their own memoirs.

They learned the broad definition of *genre*; for example, knowing the purpose of memoir helped all the students understand that they should explain the significance of a moment to their readers. But they also learned more specific, granular knowledge, such as incorporating literary devices to add descriptive details and creating more complex sentences. Language, grammar, and syntax were taught within the broader context of genre. It must be stressed that there is not an emphasis on form so that students merely mimic a piece of writing; rather, it serves as a way to discuss the "social purposes" of writing (Smagorinsky, 2008, p. 74).

This type of instruction is rare in juvenile detention centers. One reason for this is because in juvenile detention centers, writing is often taught secondary to reading. Learning how to read is often viewed as a functional skill, one that people need to have in order to operate in their daily lives. While this is true, we should not dismiss the importance of writing in people's lives. For example, narrative writing serves as an emotional outlet and a way to document life stories, and persuasive writing provides students a way to voice their opinions.

In addition, writing is a multifaceted and complex skill that takes time to develop, which seems to be why this type of instruction is not implemented in juvenile detention facilities. Teachers, however, can strategically adapt writing instruction to help students craft their writing. Using exemplary models scaffolds their students' understanding of audience, purpose, structure, and discourse. While they need a teacher's help during the initial process, the more students learn to study writing, the more they will be able to direct their own observed features of text. In addition, while they are studying writing to benefit their own process, they are learning how to read critically. Students learn how to ask questions about texts and begin to realize that authors have specific purposes when crafting writing. Writing instruction should provide students the opportunity to consider their own experiences and make connections to other texts and the world around them.

Teaching students how to write is more than simply editing grammar in sentences or evaluating how much students can write within a given time period. If we want students to grow as writers, then we need to let them write. We need to talk to them about their writing. And then we need to let them write more often and for longer periods of time.

Chapter Three

Shying Away from Sad

Identity and Writing

In *The Stories We Live By* Dan McAdams (1993) writes, "[I]f you want to know me, then you must know my story, for my story defines who I am. And if I want to know myself, to gain insight into the meaning of my own life, then I, too, must come to know my story" (p. 11). Scholars like McAdams view the stories we tell about ourselves as our identities; our identities are in fact the stories we construct about our lives. With this perspective, language is crucial in how we identify ourselves. Our stories are the gel that "hold[s] experiences together in a way that allows people to act as if they possess identities" (McCarthy & Moje, 2002, 427). Through our stories we construct our and present our identities and reject other identities.

Though identity construction is constant, popular culture portrays adolescence as the time when we really define and express who we are. We think of teenagers as deciding who they are and who they will become, but identity isn't stable. Identity is not a rough image formed in adolescence in order to achieve a particular identity in adulthood. Rather, we constantly engage in identity construction, and we represent ourselves through language, our actions toward one another and in particular situations, and how we and others view ourselves. Identity can be situational, as well, in how we choose to present and position ourselves within a given context.

While at the detention center, youths are in a unique space of identity construction. The mission of the juvenile justice system is to reform and reshape youths' lives, behaviors, and attitudes; therefore, students are not just physically confined but also mentally and emotionally confined (Abrams & Hyun, 2009; Pytash, 2014). This in itself is a traumatic experience that often

Excerpt from Suzanne's poetry notebook

influences to a great degree how adolescents are identified, how they take up identities, and which identities stay with them.

This is never as clearly evident as when youths come into the detention center classroom. They walk into and out of the classroom by calling out a number assigned to them so the guards can retain control and make sure everyone is accounted for. This strips away identity, as these young people become numbers instead of names.

Furthermore, other visible and concrete identity markers adolescents use are purposefully removed. For example, clothes, hairstyles, jewelry, and tattoos are replaced with orange and green jumpsuits. Instead of individuality there is a group of detained youths clothed in the colors and fashion of shame, trouble, and exclusion.

This conformity allows for control and punishment, and the experience of incarceration, confinement, or detainment significantly shapes youths' lives and perceptions of themselves. This experience becomes *part* of their story— *part* because this experience does not define them, as their personal identities are more resilient than the external trappings of the exclusion from society.

As teachers, our ethics require us to care for and nurture the youths in front of us. Their identities—their stories—must be important to us. Through writing instruction, we enable positive and resilient development. Teachers may be confined by the rules of detention, but we can protect, nurture, and create small spaces of personal freedom and expression.

INSTRUCTIONAL PRINCIPLES

Our instruction should acknowledge the important relationship between identity and literacy and provide youths the space to engage in self-preservation. Self-preservation allows students the dignity to maintain those aspects of themselves they want to express or project, and personal writing provides the opportunity for self-preservation.

As students negotiate their identities within their life experiences and the many spaces in which they live, we must consider how they position themselves as writers in our classrooms. Youths in detention centers have often survived incredible traumas, and when we provide them opportunities to write about their lives, these traumas might creep into their writing, which has implications for our teaching. The four design principles in this chapter are:

1. Writing to Cope. Narrative writing can serve as a gateway for students to cope with experiences and emotions.

2. Serving as a Critical Witness. Teachers should serve as critical witnesses (Dutro, 2013; Wissman & Wiseman, 2011) to the "incomprehensible" traumas in youths' lives.

3. Suspending Sadness and Reauthoring Lives. While we may serve as witnesses through their writing to the traumas in their lives, we must also recognize their strengths and resiliency factors and see the ways writing can serve as a way for students to re-author their stories.

4. Writing for Relationships. Writing allows youth to maintain relationships, even when detained.

WRITING TO COPE

Youths' experiences significantly shape their views of themselves and the world. Outside of detention facilities, youths generally face a myriad of life challenges and experience chaotic lives. Adolescents can experience homelessness, physical and sexual abuse, unwanted pregnancy, extreme poverty, drug and alcohol addictions, violent interactions with others (including law enforcement), and habitual truancy (Chesney-Lind & Shelden, 2004; Krisberg, 2005; Pytash, 2013, 2016). In addition, they often move back and forth between their homes, the detention center, group foster homes, their school, alternative schools, and community programs, so their identities are forged while navigating multiple worlds.

Maya Angelou writes, "There is no greater agony than bearing an untold story inside you." This certainly seems to be why many adolescents write. When young adults in the detention center are asked why they write in their personal lives, the answers vary, but writing for healing and coping is a consistent theme. Many adolescents reveal that they keep journals, write poetry, or compose musical lyrics to release their emotions in a safe space and to help them make sense of the unimaginable traumas they have experienced.

Libraries, hospitals, and counseling centers often encourage people to read and write as therapy, also known as bibliotherapy. Researchers of bibliotherapy who work with young adults have found that reading and writing help them to solve problems, cope with life experiences, sustain meaningful relationships, and make positive life changes (Gooding, 2008; Ihanus, 2005; Mazza, 2003; Prater, Johnstun, Dyches, & Johnstun, 2006).

When young adults compose poems, lyrics, or stories about their personal lives, they engage in a form of bibliotherapy. Their writing is a part of their healing, thinking, and coping processes. It provides space for introspective thought as they consciously or subconsciously process experiences, solve problems, and deal with stress. The complexity of their lives often appears in the topics they write about and the stories they share with others.

IN ACTION: SUZANNE

Suzanne's life was tumultuous; she had a negative and often violent relationship with her mother. All of her time in the detention center was related to domestic violence charges, including assaults against her mother and as a victim herself.

Susanne was asked to write a literacy vignette on an important moment as a reader and writer. The goal was to help Suzanne articulate why reading and writing were important in her life. Her writing became a document of her court history, including a description of when she stole cigarettes from her stepfather, leading to a physical fight between her and her mother and Suzanne's resulting arrest. Unfortunately, the violence in Suzanne's home is not unique, as state and national reports document that much of the violence girls experience or partake in is "family centered" (Chesney-Lind & Shelden, 2004, p. 54). For Suzanne, writing was a way to deal with these violent episodes:

Suzanne: Writing gets all my emotions out because if they stay all bottled in, it's not good.

Kristine: What do you mean, "it's not good"?

Suzanne: I flip out a lot.

Kristine: So writing helps you to deal with all those things and not flip out?

Suzanne: Yeah.

Later, after Suzanne was released and attending her traditional school, we sat together at the local McDonald's; while it is a convenient place to meet, we chose this spot primarily because the boy Suzanne liked worked behind the counter. We talked about writing and why it helps her deal with her emotions. Suzanne shared that she knew her mom went through her bedroom, looking for her writing. As we sat in a red plastic booth, Suzanne described when she left her mom a suicide note three years ago:

Suzanne: My mom reads all my stuff.

Kristine: She does? How do you know she does that?

Suzanne: Because when she was going through my room once, she found a suicide note that I wrote.

Kristine: Does it bother you that your mom reads your writing?

Suzanne: Yeah because I don't read her stuff.

Kristine: So do you see her going through your stuff?

Suzanne: No, I just know, and I knew it was her that took the suicide note because when I went through her room, I saw it in her drawer.

Kristine: Did you ever talk to her about it?

Suzanne: No.

Kristine: Do you ever talk to her about the writing you do?

Suzanne: No. She don't care.

Kristine: Why do you say that?

Suzanne: She doesn't. Like I try to talk to her, and she says, "Alright Suzanne, I am watching TV. Go play."

Her feelings of hurt and betrayal were obvious as she rolled her eyes and mimicked her mom. It seemed sad and slightly ironic that in a restaurant predominantly for families and children, we were having a conversation about her seemingly toxic relationship with her mother. She continued to explain that she wanted her mom to find her suicide note: "I left it right on my bed. I knew she would go through my things and find it."

A week later, I was back at McDonald's, but this time I was sitting in the parking lot talking to her mom on the phone. I asked why she thought Suzanne wrote and why she thought writing was important. Without prompting, she also brought up the suicide note: "I look at them [her poems] when she isn't there. Once, before she was on medication, she wrote about killing herself. And then I had to talk to her about that, and we got her in to see someone." Despite all of this, they never acknowledged that this was their form of communication. Suzanne's writing was an act of self-awareness that helped her not only to process her pain, but also to express her pain to others so she could receive help.

SERVING AS A CRITICAL WITNESS

It is important to note that Suzanne did not share her writing in a classroom setting. Though she talked about the benefits of writing, she did not talk about the benefits of sharing her writing with teachers or classmates. Her writing was personal and shared only when she wanted to share it. As teachers, we must recognize that our students, even those we don't typically view as writers, may be writing to deal with life circumstances, to reflect on emotional situations, or to make sense of traumatic events. Sometimes this form of coping edges into the writing classroom, leaving writing teachers to ask themselves, "How do I respond to a piece of writing that deals with a traumatic incident or feelings of pain and sorrow? What is the appropriate professional response when these stories are shared, even though this was not the intention of the writing lesson?"

Teachers are not trained psychologists nor counselors who are supposed to help heal students; therefore, personal sharing through writing can be tricky for teachers in both traditional schools and detention centers. Teachers are mandatory reporters for neglect and abuse, and in the writing workshops at detention centers, youths are reminded that they are not allowed to write about their charges and that their writing can be confiscated as evidence. Though we enact these policies to protect youths and ourselves, it creates tension because students need to have a space to cope, to heal, and to use writing as a powerful tool in their lives (Wissman & Wiseman, 2011). This is particularly true in juvenile detention facilities, as being detained and confined is traumatic. How do we not expect youths to write about the trauma they experience by living at the detention center?

Literacy scholar Elizabeth Dutro advocates that teachers can serve as a "critical witness" to the "incomprehensible" experiences students may have. This requires a supportive classroom environment that embraces the students' many life stories. Dutro (2013) suggests that serving as a critical witness sometimes begins with teachers modeling how to write about and share our own life experiences. Therefore, critical witnessing is a reciprocal relationship based on mutual trust that allows students to witness our "testimony."

Most importantly, being a critical witness means that as teachers we are encouraging students to share not only stories of happy moments but also those stories of confusion, sadness, and pain. For both teachers and students, serving as a critical witness is a risk, as it exposes both our vulnerabilities and our responsibilities to one another. Similarly, Wissman and Wiseman (2011) remind teachers the importance of following state and school protocol as mandatory reporters; however, they also urge educators to "witness the child's story, attending to the child and to the story in the moment" (p. 245).

IN ACTION: ABBY

This tension isn't easy to navigate and often is a topic presented to preservice teachers for their field experience at the detention center. Abby, a preservice teacher, facilitated a writing group with young men. She decided that for her lesson she would play an instrumental piece of music. After students listened to the song, Abby asked them to draw their responses and write descriptions of their drawings.

In her rationale for the lesson, Abby wrote, "There is no right or wrong answer or way to do things. Whatever picture the music creates in the student's head is their own perception. The possibilities of where this lesson could go seemed limitless because of all of the different perceptions students will have." In addition, Abby hoped that writing about their image would help students to think about imagery and descriptive language.

Abby entered the classroom nervous but enthusiastic. During the hour students were intently listening, drawing, and writing. While discussing the lesson in her preservice class, however, she looked defeated. It was obvious that the lesson did not go as Abby had intended.

In reality Abby wasn't disappointed with the entire lesson; in fact, only one piece of writing bothered her. It was a drawing of two boys on a road, one looking over the other as he lay in the street covered in blood. The description was about a drive-by shooting, and at the end the student wrote, "People die every day, but it doesn't mean they deserve to die."

Abby explained, "It was really hard because I was trying to find something really encouraging to say, but like, what do you say about him losing his best friend to a drive-by shooting? And this was a really tranquil song, and I was trying to create this tranquil moment, but this student put an entirely different spin on it." In response, Erin, another preservice teacher, reminded Abby, "They come to class really just wanting to write about what they want."

Abby's classmates reminded her that writing about loss and sadness is okay. Erin told Abby, "Obviously this is a story that needs to be told. He wants to tell this story. If as teachers we shy away from the topics kids want to write, then we lose an avenue for learning about what they really care about and what they really feel."

SUSPENDING SADNESS AND REAUTHORING LIVES

This is a reminder that if students are given the room to choose topics that are important to them, then writing teachers must be prepared when students write about every aspect of their lives. Teachers can even go a step further to reframe these stories as not about tragedy, but about resiliency. Teachers cannot be naïve about the social realities that shape students' lives but must recognize that students are more than one piece of writing. Many stories make up their lives. And just as teachers are encouraged not to have a deficit view of the adolescents they work with, teachers can do more than notice their pain; we can notice their strengths and abilities.

For example, Suzanne recognized the cycle of violence in the encounter with her mother, and although she stated that she was angry that her mother read her writing, she continued to leave poems and short stories for her mother to find. She even left a suicide note for her mother to find, which provided her mother the impetus to seek counseling for Suzanne. The recognition and celebration of our students' strengths can help them cope with the traumatic moments of life.

If we only pay attention to a students' pain and tragic life circumstances, then we miss the stories that have contributed to their happiness. Eve Tuck (2009), an educational researcher and reformer, makes this case about the dangers of this in an open letter to the academic community, "Suspending Damage: A Letter to Communities":

> In damage-centered research, one of the major activities is to document pain or loss in an individual, community, or tribe. Though connected to deficit models—frameworks that emphasize what a particular student, family, or community is lacking to explain underachievement or failure—damage-centered research is distinct in being more socially and historically situated. It looks to historical exploitation, domination, and colonization to explain contemporary brokenness, such as poverty, poor health, and low literacy.

As Tuck notes, feeling compassion toward our students is easy when we hear about the tragedies in their lives. Their struggles and pain are often in the foreground. When we stop and listen to their stories, it can be painful for us to see how many young adults have been used, manipulated, and disregarded by the educational, social, and political systems that often control their lives. These realities cannot be ignored, and educators must work to disrupt the systems that lead to these injustices.

However, only thinking of students as damaged or broken is dangerous. Concentrating on their pain causes us to miss their abilities, hopes, dreams, and goals. And though adolescents need opportunities to process and cope with unspeakable heartbreak, writing allows young adults to reframe and rethink their experiences, so that they can also see the possibilities in themselves and in their lives. In addition, by looking holistically at youths' lives and providing them an opportunity to voice their stories, they can reauthor their experiences and "imagine alternative possibilities for their own becoming" (Greene, 1995, p. 39).

When adolescents write about topics important to them, they give meaning to and make sense of their lives. They write poetry, lyrics, and stories to ascribe meaning to these experiences, allowing them to be metacognitive and reflective and answer the question, "Who am I?" McAdams (1993) contends, "Stories help us organize our thoughts, providing a narrative for human intentions and interpersonal events that is readily remembered and told. In some instances, stories may also mend us when we are broken, heal us when we are sick, and even move us toward psychological fulfillment and maturity" (p. 31). Therefore, the stories adolescents share about their lives in writing are constructed and reconstructed as they work to make sense of their lived experiences.

People are constantly deciding which stories fit into their perceptions of themselves and their worlds. Some experiences become dominant, and others become less important. Student writing can be a statement about how they perceive themselves and the stories they have created about their lives. But this isn't always a complete retelling of all their experiences.

Counseling researchers White and Epston (1990) define this process of reauthoring as the "process of persons' entering into stories, taking them over, and making them their own" (p. 13). Writing provides students a chance to write about their lives and therefore a chance to reauthor their experiences. In this sense, narrative writing does more than just allow them to reflect and share their life stories; writing also allows them to reconsider how they perceive themselves and their life events.

IN ACTION: JAMES AND COPING WITH LOSS

James was a regular at the detention center's writing workshop. Although most adolescents cycled in and out of the detention center, James's placements seemed to last longer than most. His final arrest as a juvenile led to his longest stay; he was to be transferred to a long-term high-security facility, but the prison didn't have the space. Until he could be transferred, he was at the detention center and therefore a consistent member of the writing workshop group.

James showed up to each writing session with a journal in hand. This was unusual, as the guards didn't typically let students bring personal possessions with them. But James's friendly demeanor and his pleas somehow convinced the guards to allow him to have his journal. Over time, James began to share his journal entries. He would talk about a poem that he wrote about his girlfriend or share that he wrote to try to understand how he got in this situation. He often shared that he wrote because he missed his dad, who died when he was one year old. Even though he had no memories of his father, he still felt a hole in his life from his absence:

> This is a letter to my dad. I don't get to talk to him 'cause he died when I was one. I never got to talk to him. So the stuff that I do, that couldn't replace him, but this is very emotional. This is like, I know my words, I know he can hear them. I know he can understand them. No one else knows where I come from, but he does. So I wrote these words down, just to get them off my chest. I just write to get things off my chest . . . things I can't tell other people.

James didn't just write to reread what he had written in his journal; he read his words aloud. In a whisper, James explained, "When I read it aloud, when I write, I don't just write stuff. I read it aloud a lot."

Kristine: Who do you read it to?

James: Myself.

Kristine: Why do you read it aloud?

James: So he can hear it

Kristine: Your dad?

James: It makes me feel like I am talking to him. It's called *A Life With Him*. When I read it, I just feel like the weight lifted off me.

It is easy to focus on James's pain and suffering, but in doing so we overlook that he learned to cope with loss and process his emotions through writing. He believed that writing formed a bond between him and his father. In some ways he didn't lose his father; instead writing gave him his father's presence, allowing him to converse with his dad and contributing to his sense of well-being.

WRITING FOR RELATIONSHIPS

Scholars of education, counseling, psychology, social work, and medicine note that social relationships are crucial during adolescence. Knowing who we are in relation to others is important for identity formation in adolescence, and youths often search for these connections and relationships. In fact, the Search Institute (2006) found that having relationships with adults who model positive and responsible behavior is vital for young adults aged 12 to 18 to be emotionally healthy and empathetic.

Researchers have documented how literacy serves as a way for young adults to establish, develop, and maintain relationships (Boyd, 2013; Finders, 1997). Studies of common, everyday literacy practices that teenagers typically engage in, such as signing yearbooks (Finders, 1997) or posting pictures on Facebook (Boyd, 2013), have found that these activities extend youths' social opportunities and networks.

Being in a detention center isolates youths from their friends, families, and communities at a time when they are in desperate need of and craving personal relationships. In fact, researchers who have surveyed young adults in juvenile detention centers found that 94% desire to remain in contact with their families (Sedlak & McPherson, 2010), even if society labels these families as dysfunctional and unhappy.

Relationships with family members are key; unfortunately, it can be difficult for family to visit because of work, school responsibilities, and other obligations during visitation days and times. Researchers have found that one-third of youths do not have face-to-face visits while detained because of time constraints and distance. For 59% of youths, it takes their families one hour of travel to visit them; for 28% it takes more than three hours (Sedlak & McPherson, 2010).

Youths often discuss how writing allows them to share their thoughts, feelings, and emotions with others. Detained youths report that they write and share poetry with girlfriends, boyfriends, mothers, fathers, siblings, and friends. Some youths explain that they have an easier time communicating their thoughts through letters rather than verbally sharing what they are feeling.

As adolescents are isolated from their social worlds in juvenile detention centers, one of their main writing practices is letter writing. While most adolescents today communicate through text messaging or social media, such as Instagram or Facebook, youths in the juvenile justice system write letters. It is so important that detention centers often dedicate time in the day to letter writing. Youths have an extended period to read letters they receive and respond to family members and friends.

Writing letters allows youths to check in with friends or to learn about events happening in their schools or communities. Not only are they interested in their families' and friends' well-being, but they also learn from their families about court appearances and release dates, which alleviates their anxiety and frustration.

Writing also allows youths to cope with traumatic events and maintain those relationships that they consider valuable to their lives, while providing self-preservation. This has implications for how we as writing teachers position youths and ourselves during the writing process. Writing should always be an act of freedom.

IN ACTION: MOLLY'S WRITING FOR RELATIONSHIPS

Molly at 15 years old was facing one of the most challenging times of her life. Growing up in a small town with a predominantly white, poverty-stricken population, Molly began experimenting with drugs out of what she called boredom. In addition, Molly's father was diagnosed with cancer, and drugs were a way to escape her anxiety and fear about her father's sickness. What was originally recreational quickly became an addiction.

Molly stopped attending school, leading to multiple suspensions. She was sent to an alternative school and then was in and out of a juvenile detention facility. In addition, her involvement in the juvenile court system for mostly drug-related offenses led her to a rehabilitation center.

Molly described herself as a passionate reader and writer, although she shared that she would "rather write my own stuff than read." She went on to explain, "I'm really inspired by what people write. I read to know there is somebody else out there, you know, that feels the same way I do. There is just somebody that just knows." One book she felt very connected to was *Heroin Diaries: A Year in the Life of a Shattered Rock Star* (Sixx, 2008), the nonfictional account of Mötley Crüe bassist Nikki Sixx's battle with drug addiction. Molly explained how the author's struggle with drug addiction reminded her of her own struggle with drugs. She also appreciated how the book included "poetry and a lot of song lyrics." Her need to find others with similar experiences came through in her writing. She consistently discussed writing as a way to cope with frustrations and anger; however, her writing wasn't a completely private endeavor.

One afternoon, I talked with Molly's mom and brother about why she liked to write. Her new puppy Zoe ran circles around the living room. As she picked up the dog, her mom began to talk about writing as a way for Molly to vent. Rocking in her recliner, she looked at Molly, then at me, and said, "I think it makes her happy when she writes. It makes her feel better. Like, she don't talk, but she writes." Her brother, folding and unfolding his hands, agreed: "I think it's just easier for her to put her feelings on paper."

Later, when we were sitting in her the library of her school, which has just 300 students in grades 9 through 12, Molly wrote a literacy vignette about a moment when writing was particularly important to her. She wrote without stopping. Eventually she looked up and explained that a few years prior, her bother left her a poem about their lives and growing up together. She was touched by the poem and shared it with her mom, who encouraged Molly to also write a poem to him in response, which led them to have an intimate literary conversation that was really important to Molly because "It made me realize how he felt about me. It was a time that we were actually starting to have conversations with each other. My brother is my hero."

For Molly, writing the literacy vignette was a reauthoring of this particular experience. Her brother and her mom knew personal, intimate details of her life through her writing, and this piece was a reflection on how writing has always created bonds.

⬤⬤⬤ Around three years' when I came home from a friends I came to find a piece of white paper folde. neatly on my table. I stared in Curiosity, because this piece of paper said To: From; I sat down unfolded the paper, and I began to read. As I read this beautiful piece of work, tears started to overpower my e; It was a poem to me, from my brother. I read this poem continuou: because it made me feel rather special. Just to know that my brother cared, and all the good he knew I had within. The poem made me happy for that reas. out said because he talked about us gr. up. I wasn't so sure if wanted anyone else to read it only because it was or me.

Molly's vignette, page 1

CONCLUSION

Identity is dynamic and fluid, constantly shifting and being constructed. Youths in detention centers are in a precarious situation; they are engaged in self-preservation of their identities while being labeled by society.

I couldnt keep it to myself. I walked downstairs, where my mother was sitting in the Rocking chair watching TV. She asked me "why are you crying, whats wrong." I replied "Nothings wrong, eft me a poem ☺." My mother read the poem and she smiled. ~~She~~ ~~~~ She said "That's very good, maybe you

Molly's vignette, page 2

Writing is intricately woven into our identities in how we choose to narrate our experiences and the stories we share with others. At the detention center, writing can serve as resistance against the labeling youths receive from the outside world. Writing can also serve as a reminder of the relationships that have formed their identities. In this sense, writing is an extension of their identities.

When youths write about their personal lives, they tend to write about their experiences in order to cope, explore, and share. As teachers, we don't intentionally create assignments for students to engage in therapeutic writing. However, we do provide opportunities for students to share their lives, and because of this, we learn that writing is important for voicing the happy, sad, frustrating, and exciting experiences. At the end of the semester, Abby had the following reflection:

> When I first came here, I was sad because you just would hear such sad stories. But now I feel a little differently. Last week one of the students told me that he was leaving in two days. And he said that his grandma was picking him up and they had plans to go into the city. So yeah, their stories are sad, but I also see the positives in their lives. And it's not the end for them. They still have a future.

returned from work, and I
heard him come in, he stopped to
talk to my mom, so I crept quitly into
his room, and sat the paper on his dress
I went back into my room and waited
very patiently. I heard footsteps coming
from outside my door, a slight knock
then the door opened. My brother walkec
in, sat down beside me, then gave me
a hug. We talked for almost two whole
hours. about our life, about what wr
wanted to be. We planned everything
out. I'm not so sure if it was
poetry that brought us closer togethe
or if we both were maturing at
that time. whatever it was, that da
I learned things about my brother,
that he cared a whole lot for me,
and that one of his interests were
also mine. ☺

Molly's vignette, page 3

Chapter Four

"Sometimes Gun Violence Is Good"

Attorneys should take more time to earn a child's trust as they build a more accurate defense, prosecution, and inquiry. Because there is no doubt, youths are more likely to be wrongfully convicted than adults. For example, "False confessions are one of the leading causes of wrongful convictions, accounting for roughly 25% of all convictions that were later overturned based on DNA evidence." But even more shockingly, "One leading study of 125 proven false confession cases found that 63% of false confessors were under the age of twenty-five and 32% were under the age of eighteen" (Bluhn Legal Clinic).

* * *

Evidence-based writing is considered persuasive or argumentative, requiring students to gather evidence to support their ideas. After students adopt a position on a particular topic, they must read multiple viewpoints on the subject and decide if what they are learning from their reading reinforces their ideas. Students are engaged in multiple acts of critical thinking when using evidence to support their ideas: (1) They develop a firm understanding of their beliefs and viewpoints; (2) they learn to evaluate sources when reading; and (3) they discern the most important evidence that supports their ideas. Students also learn how to weave this evidence throughout their writing.

An increased emphasis is placed on evidence-based writing instruction because we assume it aligns with the writing students do at the college and career levels. Nonetheless, evidence-based writing is important for other reasons as well. It encourages students to go beyond stating their ideas to learning to support their ideas and make convincing arguments—critical analysis that can help youths develop their identities as meaning makers.

Newell, Bloome, and Hirvela (2015) explain, "[T]eaching students to write an argument is not a technical matter, but a matter of socializing students to act, think, value, feel, and use language in particular ways that are shared with others" (p. 19). Students develop an awareness of how to construct an argument, how to use writing to generate new ideas, and how to understand and situate writing in a larger purpose and social context.

Although there are many benefits of evidence-based writing, it can be challenging to teach. Students must have significant background knowledge that they can call on. In addition, in order to collect evidence, students must engage in deep reading about their topic. This requires students not only to comprehend complex texts but also to discern why certain information supports an argument or stance. Finally, students must know how to structure a compelling argument or persuasive piece. Overall, evidence-based writing requires a nuanced understanding of a topic of interest, significant reading comprehension skills, and rhetorical knowledge.

INSTRUCTIONAL PRINCIPLES

As we reflect on all of the necessary elements to craft evidence-based writing, teachers must also consider how we engage students in writing instruction to help them become critical thinkers and problem solvers. This is complicated because in order to draft evidence-based writing, students need knowledge of content, genre features, and language used in argumentative or persuasive writing. This leads to three design principles:

1. Teacher Listening and Student Choice. Students need opportunities to write about topics that are interesting and relevant to them. As teachers we cannot be afraid to have our students write about the important social issues in their lives. It requires us to take a position as a learner of the interplay between youths' choice and representation of social issues.

2. Authentic Genres and Conversations About Genre. Evidence-based writing does not have to be relegated to a five-paragraph essay. Students are knowledgeable of many argumentative and persuasive genres and should have opportunities to write in the genres that are familiar and relevant.

3. Deconstructing Writing. Students critically analyze the genre, beginning with a close examination of purpose and audience. When they know why they are reading and toward whom to direct their writing, they are better prepared to craft their pieces. By carefully studying writing, students begin to notice how argumentative and persuasive pieces are structured. This requires students to ask questions while reading in order to deconstruct how the genre is crafted.

TEACHER LISTENING AND STUDENT CHOICE

Evidence-based writing must be personally relevant, engaging, and motivating. This happens when we allow students to write about issues that are important to their lives and communities. While this seems simple in theory, we have to learn to carefully listen to our students and discern their points of view. Teachers must ask questions about why topics are important to students and take time to listen to their responses. It is not enough to acknowledge students' topics and then move to instruction. We must carefully consider *why* a student is drawn to a particular topic and acknowledge the institutional factors that might drive students' and our own belief systems.

When students select the topics they want to write about, teachers position the students to become experts. Students are not merely passive recipients of knowledge. They are viewed as having "funds of knowledge" (Moll, Amanti, Neff, & Gonzalez, 1992), their beliefs and experiences forming the foundation for their writing. Teachers become writing mentors who can help students shape personal knowledge and disseminate their beliefs and experiences.

Meaningful writing instruction, therefore, begins with youths' voices. By truly listening to our students, we refrain from making assumptions about what they perceive as relevant to and important in their lives. When we develop relationships with or live in the same community as our students, it is tempting to assume that we know about their lives and what they value. However, being writing teachers means we first must be listeners.

IN ACTION: LAMAR

The cognitive-behavioral therapy (CBT) group was designed as a "last chance" remediation for boys who were repeat offenders. The hope was that by creating a program specifically for repeat offenders and providing additional therapy, counseling, and programs while in detention, they might be able to turn their lives around when they were released. The additional programing for the CBT group included a project called Writing for Social Change. Led by me and Matt, a preservice teacher from my program, the goal for the project was to engage the youths in the CBT group in inquiry by exploring issues that they believed to be crucial in their lives and their communities. They would then examine their issues through various forms of writing, including screenplays, poetry, public service announcements, and TED Talks.

During the project, instruction was designed with three goals for helping students to engage in critically literate ways. First, the project was inquiry-based; students were encouraged to ask a question about an important issue in their community in order to build their connection to the community; to see themselves as active members with the community; and to connect their topics to a broader social context by reading relevant position statements, news articles, and commentaries. By asking a question, students would pose a solution and then be guided to look for support for their ideas.

Second, the youth were encouraged to read from a variety of sources. This was a challenge at the detention center because they were not allowed to access the Internet and could not freely select the articles they wanted to read. We provided them with information from multiple sources, so the students had access to competing viewpoints on the topic, although they were filtered through our lenses. While students were reading, they were also using annotation and note-taking strategies to help them process the information. Writing summaries and answering prompts helped them not only to read and write for comprehension but also to question and critically analyze what they were reading. And finally, youths were asked to create compositions using both traditional print and digital media that would reflect their understanding and opinions of their topics.

Lamar was a member of the CBT group, and similar to most of the boys in the group, he was black and 16 years old. Lamar immediately stated that his issue would be that "sometimes gun violence is good." Later, toward the end of the project, when asked why he chose that topic, he said, "That's like what I grew up to. It's something I face every day." Initially, Lamar did not want to write, and at times during the project, he was resistant and disengaged but only to the extent that he would not lose the other boys' attention.

However, Lamar was very interested in using the Nexus 7 tablets available to students during the project, and he asked if he could create a video about gun violence. As part of his video composition, Lamar asked if he could interview the other boys, the guards, and Matt. During many of the interviews, Lamar would hold up the tablet and say to the person, "Tell me about gun violence." Typically, these interviews quickly moved off topic. Everyone interviewed responded that guns and gun violence were bad. No one took Lamar's interviews seriously, especially the guards, who felt that Lamar was being unproductive and disruptive. They would tell Lamar to "cut it out" and typically voiced their frustration that Lamar was moving too much around the classroom to make his video.

Lamar finished his video; it was 14 minutes and 53 seconds long. It didn't include any of his annotated evidence from his reading. Even more interesting is that he didn't include any of the interviews. Most of the video was actually Lamar filming himself and using applications on the tablet to create effects, which resulted in a final product that was visually interesting but didn't address any of his findings.

Lamar's decision not to use any of the interviews was the most interesting conundrum because he insisted on conducting them. When asked about this,

Lamar replied, "Everyone was fake. Everyone said guns are bad, but everyone don't really believe that."

His comment about everyone being fake served as a major catalyst for a change. We realized that our instructional goals were compromised by our execution. While it may not be considered socially acceptable to claim that gun violence is good, for Lamar that was very much his truth, as he explained that it was something that he "faced every day." Lamar needed to be reengaged in his topic.

The goal was to get Lamar involved in this process, and so it began with a conversation. We talked about why people would argue that citizens have a right to have weapons. We talked about organizations, such as the National Rifle Association, and Lamar seemed surprised to read position statements supporting people's rights to have guns. Lamar also read additional pieces about gun violence from a variety of sources, including the Coalition to Stop Gun Violence.

We talked about who would author such pieces, why, and who the readers would be. We provided Lamar with multiple viewpoints so he could use that information to make his decision about the issue, while keeping in mind his personal experiences. Reading a variety of viewpoints about gun violence seemed to help Lamar to think about how his beliefs connected to others, and he began freewriting about his experiences.

Lamar started each session by writing, which became a metareflective exercise. Some of his freewriting pieces he shared; others he did not. Through the pieces he shared, it seemed as if Lamar was thinking about what he believed and was starting to recognize how his life experiences might shape his feelings. His writing indicated that he was conflicted about guns, something he admitted as well. For example, he wrote about a friend who was killed in a drive-by outside his home. Lamar wrote about another friend who was in prison because he killed someone with a gun. He realized that guns could both offer him protection and lead to his demise. He connected his experiences to the experiences of members in his community:

> I'm tired of my family dying of guns. I'm tired of friends dying of guns. I keep one to protect me and my family and friends. So I can't be mad at all if I die by one. My friend Jason was shot and killed on his porch while his grandma was in the house. On the other hand, my friend got sentenced to 40 years at the age of 17, and now he is gone and will be in jail for a long, long time. His life is also over because of a gun.

His inquiry statement shifted from "Gun violence is good" to "Should people be allowed to have guns?" He started to question if gun violence was something different from whether people should have the right to own guns. Through the drafting of his ideas, it became obvious that his beliefs about guns were based on the complexity of his experiences. Lamar didn't complete a final finished version of any of his pieces, but we witnessed his critical thinking about this particular societal issue, as well as a recognition that writing might be able to help him sort through his ideas, feelings, and experiences.

AUTHENTIC GENRES AND CONVERSATIONS ABOUT GENRE

While we work to understand why a student selects a particular topic to write about, we must also think about how students will represent their topics through writing. Engaging students in conversations about social issues is powerful when teachers incorporate authentic genres of evidence-based writing in the classroom. Genres are how we classify text based on similar features (e.g., historical fiction, news articles, or poetry). Too often in schools, we fail to teach students about the writing they might encounter in their everyday lives or within particular disciplines.

Students view writing as a five-paragraph essay instead of a particular way of communicating with others. Therefore, in order to have conversations about how and why authors write, teachers can include reading and writing genres that are not artificially created for school purposes but are actual ways people write.

Two popular genres that could be considered persuasive or argumentative are public service announcements (PSAs) and TED Talks. PSAs are used to promote specific agendas and sway people to think and act in a certain way. Examples abound, from Smokey the Bear's "Only you can prevent forest fires" and the Partnership for a Drug-Free America's "This is your brain on drugs" campaigns to the more recent PSAs about the dangers of texting and driving. PSAs allow for conversations about how people are persuaded not only through rhetoric but also through the use of images and audio. This helps students to think carefully about how messages are constructed and conveyed.

TED Talks are short speeches devoted to promoting ideas about a range of topics, which typically includes a mix of storytelling with persuasive strategies. Often people listen to a TED Talk because they are interested in the topic; however, analyzing a TED Talk helps students to become cognizant of the craft of writing.

When teachers introduce genres, we should have explicit conversations with students so they can gain insight into the genre, why an author would convey a message in this way, and who might be reading the genre. Writing teachers can prompt students to be analytical about genre by asking provocative questions, such as

1. Why did the author include this piece in a news article or blog post or on social media?
2. Are there images included in the writing? If so, what are they, and how does the author refer to them during the written piece?
3. Why would an author choose this particular form of writing to disseminate ideas about this particular topic?

These go beyond asking questions about the content (e.g., What is the piece about?) and prompt students to be critical thinkers about why someone might write in a particular way. This also pushes students toward asking questions about the written form and structure of the piece (e.g., Why did this author choose to disseminate knowledge and ideas in this way?).

IN ACTION: AMANDA'S PRO AND CON OP-ED INSTRUCTION

Amanda (featured in chapter 3) wanted to introduce students to persuasive writing. Specifically, she decided to have them study newspaper opinion and editorial pieces. She found pieces from the *Los Angeles Times* that were pro and con editorials. The opening paragraphs introduced readers to a controversial topic, and then two experts responded.

Amanda began the unit by reading aloud to students a pro and con piece of lowering the drinking age. She then asked students, "Why would someone want to read an article that told people varying ways to think about an important topic?" Students responded about knowing "both sides of an argument" or that someone might "want a lot of information before making a decision."

Amanda continued the lesson by thinking aloud as she read the piece, stopping to highlight where each author used evidence to support ideas. She also pointed out places where authors used historical references to support their points. For example, the author arguing for lowering the drinking age referenced prohibition in the 1920s. Amanda also noted that authors referenced their personal beliefs with such statements as "I advocate" and "I have no problem."

After Amanda's thinking aloud, she returned to the broader conversation about the pro and con op-ed genre. She asked the class, "We thought about why someone might want to read this genre, but why would someone want to write a pro or con about a particular topic? Why would you want your opinions right next to someone's completely opposite opinions?" One student responded, "Maybe the other person doesn't have as good of an argument, and so that makes your ideas seem better than theirs." Another student explained, "Because then people see both sides and can figure out that your ideas make more sense." The students began to see the pro and con genre as a type of writing competition to win an audience.

Amanda brainstormed with students about topics that they might want to write and debate. For example, students selected such topics as "Should the age of cigarette buying be raised?" and "Do video games make kids violent?"

Deshawn and Demitri decided to write persuasive pieces in response to the prompt "Does boredom lead to trouble, and should communities be responsible for hosting positive activities for kids?" Deshawn argued that boredom was a reason that youths get into trouble. In his persuasive piece, he argued, "If neighborhoods had different types of activities during the summer, kids would participate and wouldn't be bored. For example, kids need summer sports leagues, such as football, basketball, baseball, soccer, kickball, and volleyball." He used evidence from the Afterschool Alliance (2012) report to argue, "There is no funding for kids who really need it as 'the greatest challenges are those . . . from high-poverty and low-performing schools.'" Demitri, on the other hand, argued that just having options for youths during the summer wasn't a guarantee that they would participate: "Even when there are things to do in my community, there are still kids getting in trouble."

When asked after to reflect on their writing, Deshawn and Demitri both were able to articulate that the goal for persuasive writing is to convince readers using personal experiences and evidence from sources.

DECONSTRUCTING WRITING

Explicit conversations are important to have with students so they can observe how authors craft writing with evidence to argue or persuade others. Students need to consider not only what authors write but also how they structure their writing and the forms in which they choose to write.

Creating Lists of Observations

As noted in earlier chapters, teachers can engage students in critically analyzing writing by positioning students to *read like writers*. For example, in TED Talks, speakers typically begin with a story or vignette. This is the hook to draw the viewer into the speech. Most TED Talks then present an idea followed by evidence to support the idea. Often speakers present a counterclaim but quickly reject the claim. Speakers might finish the TED Talk by going back to the opening vignette to solidify their point.

In addition to noticing the content, a teacher can also point out to students how speakers use language. For example, TED Talks are intended to be accessible to a wide audience with differing backgrounds. Some speeches may focus on a specific discipline, such as science, and the speaker may use domain-specific terminology or jargon; however, the speaker will often use such phrases as *that means* or *this suggests* to translate a term.

A teacher can also highlight instances in which authors use evidence. This can lead to conversations about how quality evidence supports claims, which begins the exploration of how persuasive and argumentative genres are structured. This also helps students to become more critical consumers—to look for ways they are swayed by others' arguments and how they might persuade others.

While this process begins with a teacher modeling thinking, it also includes opportunities for collaboration and independent work. This process may take time, but it must happen before students begin writing.

Analytical Reading for Evidence to Support Ideas

Once students have a sense of how to construct the genre, they must do additional analytical readings to gather support for their claims. Teaching students how to construct persuasive or argumentative writing is challenging because they must extend their writing past their own experiences to also including research that will help them to create a compelling piece. As students read other people's ideas, they must look for bias, a nuance of reading analytically and critically. Such strategies as annotating and asking questions about text can guide students to understand the type of evidence available, as well as the manner in which an author presents data or information.

Powerful writing comes from students who are analytical and thoughtful as they connect their lives to a universe of ideas. Analytical reading can help students to justify and reinforce their ideas, or it can help them to rethink a topic. Students make connections by realizing that other people have similar experiences or thoughts about the world. It also helps them to ask authentic, situated questions, such as:

- Is this topic a local concern?
- How does this connect to more global issues?
- How are other people handling and resolving these issues?
- What are solutions that I haven't considered?
- How might my thinking help someone else?

Often this complex process is new to students at the detention center and requires teacher scaffolding through the reading, thinking, and writing processes. However, doing so will help students to think flexibly about the issues of which they are concerned. They learn to consider multiple viewpoints and analyze why they have certain beliefs. In addition, students begin to realize they are not isolated in their views on the world.

IN ACTION: GEORGE

The What If Program engages youths on probation and preservice teachers in conversations, reading, and writing about community issues and using digital media to learn more, compose, and perform TED Talks. What If was held once a week for two hours. Every session started with a "Writing Into the Day," a ten-minute opening in which everyone wrote. Preservice teachers took the responsibility of leading the "Writing Into the Day" time together; sometimes this was open-ended, but other times the group was more focused on the writing. This time was very important to the writing process, as it provided brainstorming sessions to help group members consider topics they felt passionate enough about to sustain them through the process of researching and writing their TED Talks. The remainder of the time together was used to research, write, and collaborate. For example, we watched TED Talks, and using the Reading Like a Writer framework (Smith, 1983) we deconstructed the talks.

George, a white 17-year-old male, was a member of What If. In the first session, we learned that George was fanatical about Harry Potter. With a gold-and-maroon Harry Potter scarf around his neck, even in mid-May, and a Harry Potter coffee cup always in hand, George was a Harry Potter enthusiast. It seemed like one of the reasons George gravitated to the Harry Potter stories is because he, like Harry, was an outsider. George had been in and out of group homes and foster homes. He had few friends that he spoke of, and yet, he seemed to crave acceptance. It was as if this need to be loved was why he faithfully attended What If. George explained that his favorite part of What If wasn't just being able to read and write, which he loved to do, but also having other people to talk to who were genuinely happy to have him around.

George decided to focus his inquiry on the juvenile justice system. Specifically, he shaped his inquiry to focus on the following questions: "What do young adults need from the juvenile justice system? What works? What helps young adults to make their lives better?" George's experiences taught him firsthand the complexity of the juvenile justice system as an institution.

He shared instances from his life and conveyed the understanding that juvenile justice courts did punish youths; however, George also talked about how the institutions were supposed to provide protection for youths, like in instances of child abuse or trafficking, when the court acted as a protector for youths.

George drew on his experiences and also shared his best friend's experiences. He felt like she was very much a victim of the juvenile justice system. According to George, she was physically abused at home. The court removed her from her home and placed her in a group home, where she also witnessed and experienced abuse. Knowing that someone had experienced various

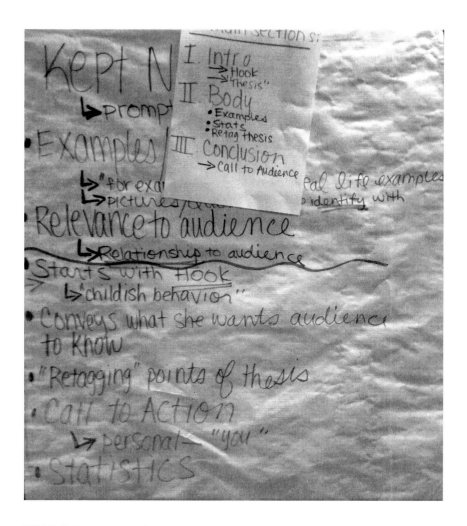

TED Talk deconstructed

forms of abuse while being "protected" by the juvenile court system made George think that juveniles should have more rights surrounding the decisions about where they live and who they live with. Through these conversations he decided that his argument was that youths did not have enough rights within the court system.

Both George and his friend were living in group homes, and George openly expressed his dislike of living in a group home. He spoke very emotionally and powerfully about his friend's experience with abuse in a group home. When there is abuse or danger in the home, often the child is removed. The child—the victim—is displaced and their lives are upended, while the perpetrator retains the right to have an uninterrupted life. George explained that he understood the rationale, but he still viewed this as unfair and traumatic.

George had a strong topic for his TED Talk and was able to draw on his and his friend's experiences to create an argumentative statement and justify his rationale for why young adults should have more rights within the juvenile justice system. He had anecdotal evidence that was heart-wrenching, but we also wanted him to have outside evidence to support his position. Our goal as writing teachers was to teach him how to critically read and find external and independent evidence to support his position. We also wanted to teach George how to strategically use both the anecdotal evidence from his life and the evidence from outside readings in his TED Talk to make a compelling argument.

George located resources and evidence to support his point of view. For example, he read about why youths are often wrongfully convicted and found statistics about the juvenile justice system and its laws and practices. George worked closely with Katie, one of the preservice teachers, and she taught him to annotate articles. This strategy helped him to identify important points within the text. Katie directed him to ask questions about what authors were saying, to highlight parts he thought were important, and to note what he found confusing while reading. Annotating each article was helpful because George gathered evidence to support his ideas while also gaining insight into how authors present information, make arguments, and persuade readers. When George found evidence he thought would be helpful in his TED Talk, we asked him to consider what the author was saying and if there was any evidence that the author cited that would be helpful in supporting his ideas. We also tried to find original sources or statistics to make sure the author's interpretation was accurate. In addition, reading texts closely to gather evidence also provided George the opportunity to weigh different perspectives and the nuanced ways evidence is used in writing.

The piece that opens this chapter is an excerpt of George's argument for why attorneys within the juvenile justice system must be more in tune with their clients' experiences and how those experiences can influence trials for young adults. While locating evidence helped George's TED Talk to become more credible, it also validated George's belief that there are problems with the juvenile justice system that need to be reformed.

CONCLUSION

When reflecting on how to teach students to write, particularly evidence-based writing in which we allow them to self-select topics, Lamar's story is an incredible reminder of the complexity of teaching writing. The reality is that Lamar was right; everyone dismissed him and his project as a serious enterprise. It isn't socially acceptable to claim that gun violence is a good thing for communities. In addition, everyone was so engrossed in his behavior and insistence that gun violence was good that we all failed to honestly engage in dialogue about his question.

As teachers and facilitators, we were working to keep everyone on course and were very dismissive of Lamar. The guards were also dismissive and didn't take his work seriously. Additionally, Lamar probably considered that the other boys' answers were fake, as he knew them personally. He recognized that being monitored for their behavior and conversations in the jail setting meant that they were probably not comfortable sharing their personal opinions. We failed Lamar. We failed to take him seriously, we failed to listen to his voice, and we failed to recognize his experience. Our beliefs about what was appropriate dictated what we wanted him to read and write. Our instructional goal was to engage Lamar in a socially conscious way, and when he tried to explore these ideas, we shut him down.

As teachers, we needed to examine our biases, blindness, and privilege. For example, what were my assumptions about guns and violence in communities? Because of the conversations, I recognized that I had strong opinions about a topic that I had never actually lived or experienced. As a white, female, middle-class teacher and researcher, I had good intentions (Milner & Laughter, 2015) for engaging students in inquiry about important issues within their communities, but we did not acknowledge the systemic social injustices that account for such issues as gun violence. For example, high concentrations of gun violence typically occur in cities that have faced years of racial segregation and poverty. We weren't asking Lamar critical questions about his experiences during our instruction. For example, Why were guns so easy for him to access? Who were the people perpetrating gun violence, and who in the community were victims or witnesses? What are the broader, historical trends of gun violence in cities?

For Lamar, gun violence was a reality that he had to confront every day. And as a black, adolescent male, he was penned in a detention center; he would eventually have a court file trailing him when he returned to his community. Being in the detention center and exploring this issue forced us to confront the injustices related to race, poverty, and violence. Lamar didn't need evidence from reading about the role of gun violence in his community. He didn't need statistics to help him understand how devastating it is to lose someone to gun violence. He didn't need a book or policy statement to explain why owning a gun might make someone feel safe. Lamar was the evidence, the living proof, that gun violence was a crucial issue within his community. By conducting interviews with teachers, guards, and fellow detained youths—those he knew were also affected by gun violence—he was gathering evidence in his own way.

Lamar forced important questions about instructional design and teaching execution. For example, How do teachers move students to think critically about their experiences? How do teachers not only empower students to speak their truths but also provide ways for them to critically explore their truths? How do teachers recognize when they have hurt their students, when they have become the oppressors by dismissing student voices? How do teachers recognize that their own assumptions and biases influence what we do in the classroom? How do they reengage students after recognizing their failures?

These are tough questions to tackle because there is not one correct answer. We cannot be afraid to have our students write about the important social issues in their lives. It requires us to take a position as a learner as we try to understand the interplay between youths' selection of social issues and how they choose to represent these issues.

Youths need to write about their lives—especially those who are detained or marginalized in schools and society—but we have to accept that their lives are complicated, and like all people, they have complex views of the world. They have learned their truths about the world, and their experiences will shape what they will want to write about. This also requires us to reexamine our own beliefs and to embrace that their beliefs may be fundamentally different from ours.

While Lamar wrote about gun violence and George wrote about the juvenile justice system, other boys wrote about such issues as the importance of graffiti in communities, the role of music in communities, and the effects of peer pressure. A colleague once commented that these were not overtly political topics; particularly she wondered why no one researched race and incarceration. This was an important point for reflection. Music in communities, for instance, is not an *overtly* political issue, so others may not view the project as crucial. Youths select topics that are important and relevant in the context of their day-to-day lives, and they wanted to voice their opinions.

Educators may assume that youths in a detention facility would want to learn and write more about societal issues that directly impact their lives, as Lamar and George did, or such topics as race and the juvenile justice system; however, we would be narrow-minded to presume that these are the only topics that affect their lives. Although the youths are living the reality of race and incarceration, this does not necessarily mean that they want to pursue these topics or that they are motivated to share their experiences and beliefs through writing. As teachers we must allow youths to choose topics they feel are interesting, important, and relevant in their lives rather than confining students to writing about topics that we assume are interesting, important, and relevant.

In an environment where youths are physically, mentally, and emotionally confined, literacy, or reading and writing, must be an act of freedom.

Despite the scholarship devoted to the importance of connecting students' lives to curriculum in ways that increase their chances for academic success and their abilities to ask critical questions, this approach is noticeably absent from classrooms in juvenile detention centers. In fact, these instructional approaches clash with the very nature of the juvenile justice system, a system built on confinement and control.

Although freedom of choice and expression of identity conflict with the culture of most juvenile justice facilities, teachers need to advocate for students and for literacy as a civil right. When we provide students with the space to bring their lives into the classroom and to see how literacy is relevant to their lives, we give them the opportunity to take ownership of their education, which is crucial to youths in juvenile detention centers. When students claim their education, they see their lives and their learning as important and relevant.

Writing is a way for youths to preserve their identities and to see the value in themselves, their cultures, and their communities. Writing instruction can create a space for teachers to bring students' lives and voices into the detention center classroom. Writing provides opportunities for youths to be known and to have their experiences, voices, and opinions validated. It is a way to locate themselves, their ideas, and their communities in the broader world through the texts they are reading.

Students need to move past replicating knowledge to demonstrating their knowledge through writing. This allows them to contribute to larger conversations about important topics in their lives, their communities, and our world. This positions them as knowledgeable members of our society and provides insight into how they represent themselves through writing.

In order for this to happen, teachers must first value students' education in juvenile detention facilities. This requires us to value their lives, their experiences, and their communities and demonstrate this value by letting them write about their lives and interests. Second, teachers must teach youths to be critical readers of multiple sources about the topics they are interested in so that they have multiple viewpoints to inform their thoughts and connections. In addition, language and discourse practices and genre structures teach them to more critically evaluate sources. In turn, they learn that writers have bias and can use evidence to persuade others. This teaches youths the power in rhetoric.

Chapter Five

The Art of Composing and Reconceptualizing Writing

Alone and no one in sight.
Coldhearted darkness is life.
Young and fearless people tell me.
But secrets show My heart is old.
Deep blue is what's really told.
Hungry for love and a wonderful soul.
Murmurs from people make me yell.
Beautiful dreams I never tell.
Thirst for red but blue is held.

* * *

Children often learn to write through drawing and intentional scribbling (Harste, Woodward, & Burke, 1984), and yet, at some point during children's schooling experiences, alphabetic print text becomes privileged. We begin to home in on students' capabilities for using alphabetic text to communicate ideas and equate literacy with the ability to read and write print-based, alphabetic text. However, scholars contend that people communicate through various modes of meaning-making. For example, Cope and Kalantzis (2009) define seven modes:

1. Written language
2. Oral language
3. Visual representation
4. Audio representation
5. Tactile representation
6. Gestural representation
7. Spatial representation

According to Cope & Kalantzis (2009), "each of these different modes has the capacity to express many of the same kinds of things; they also have representational potentials that are unique unto themselves" (p. 363). Therefore, what we might express in written language is different from what we might express through a visual mode. And each mode has certain affordances. For example, some things are more effectively communicated via image than descriptive language, while other things are more effectively communicated via print than via video. And yet, modes are often codependent and can be mixed to create new meanings. Horror movies, for example, are a great example of how sound and visual effects work together to contribute to the emotion of the film.

Scholars use the term *multimodal* to refer to the combination of multiple modes to convey meaning. Stemming from social semiotics theory, multimodality is based on the perspective that communication is "socially motivated and situated" (Bazalgette & Buckingham, 2013, p. 98). We gain meaning from events based on experiences and interactions. Scholars of social semiotic theory are interested in the variety of modes people use to communicate in particular social settings and situations. When students have the opportunity to combine multiple modes, they examine the relationships between modes and how they create new meaning when used together.

Jewitt (2008) explains, "[D]esign refers to how people make use of the resources that are available at a given moment in a specific communicational environment to realize their interests as sign makers" (p. 252). This analytical framework considers the "importance of multimodal resources, the sign maker's social purpose and intentions, context, and audience" (Jewitt, 2008, p. 252). It is helpful to think of students as composers, particularly when they compose with digital tools. While scholars argue that all texts are multimodal and that "language is a multimodal event" (Harste, Woodward, & Burke, 1984, 37), attending to such issues as font design and page layout (Kress & van Leeuween, 1996), new technologies provides affordances for digital compositions using multiple modes.

Technology is ubiquitous, changing how people write, where people write, and how people share and read writing. Students are expected to use word-processing software to write and revise their work. Online platforms, such as Google Docs, Tumblr, and Blogger, allow people to collaboratively write and share their writing. With ease, people can communicate by tweeting or posting to social media for millions to read, highlighting the recursive relationship between technology and writing that allows for creative means for communication.

New digital platforms and technological tools influence the writing classroom—the types of writing we ask students to compose and the expectations we have about their composition process. Leu and colleagues (2013) state:

Thus, to have been literate yesterday, in a world defined primarily by relatively static book technologies, does not ensure that one is fully literate today where we encounter new technologies such as Google Docs, Skype, iMovie, Contribute, Basecamp, Dropbox, Facebook, Google, Foursquare, Chrome, educational video games, or thousands of mobile apps. To be literate tomorrow will be defined by even newer technologies that have yet to appear and even newer discourses and social practices that will be created to meet future needs. (p. 1150–51)

As we consider what it means to be literate today and what it will mean to be literate in the future, we must keep in mind the many implications for how we use technology to teach writing in schools and acknowledge the sophisticated thinking students must attend to while composing digitally.

Because technology and digital media add options when students are composing, it is now easy to use computer programs, web-based platforms, and apps to incorporate various digital modes, such as visual, audio, and gestural, in a composition. While the physical act of combining modes may be easier, digital composition still requires students to be engaged in complex thinking. Students must make decisions about where images, video, and alphabetic text appear on the screen and when it is appropriate to incorporate audio files. These are not minor details that students must consider; rather these decisions call students to decide how they will design, present, and communicate ideas, knowledge, and meaning.

Technology also allows students to mix already-produced compositions and reconceptualize them to create a new piece. Through appropriating media content, students are engaging in a sophisticated process—they have to understand a text's original use and meaning and be able to reformat it into something original. As authors they must think about the purpose of their compositions and how using particular modes conveys certain meaning. They also must consider their audience's knowledge and how they will understand the composition as a whole. In fact, because digital compositions can be so readily shared with a broad audience, students must carefully consider how they will produce a composition that clearly articulates their purpose and attends to the audience viewing their work.

However, a disconnect exists between the advancement of technology and writing instruction in school. Applebee and Langer (2012) studied writing instruction in 20 middle and high schools and found that technology was often used to "reinforce" teacher-centered instructional practices for writing. For example, technology was primarily used so that students could type their papers. When teachers incorporated technology into writing instruction in innovative ways, they found that instruction was more engaging and accessible for student learning. Students have also echoed the call for the creative integration of technology in writing instruction. The Pew Internet Research Organization (Lenhart, Arafeh, Smith, & Rankin Macgill, 2008) found that

78% of adolescents surveyed thought their writing would be improved by using technology-based writing tools.

The disconnect between technology access and use in education settings most certainly extends into juvenile detention center classrooms. When youths are detained, they rarely have access to technology, let alone the latest digital tools. Youths in juvenile detention centers are typically not allowed to access the Internet, as it is viewed as a security risk. They also rarely have opportunities to use computers beyond virtual schooling and computer-supported assessments. During a lesson in which youths at a detention center had the opportunity to use a tablet, one young man stated, "I've been in here so long, so many times, I don't even know how to use these things." Tension exists with the use of technology in jail, specifically in regards to issues of safety and privacy; however, it is important to remember that outside of the detention center, youths receive the majority of their information from online sources.

As teachers, we need to explore options that allow detained students opportunities to use technology so they continue learning to communicate their ideas through digital tools and media. Our goal is for students to not only develop proficiency but also a fluency of using new media and digital tools to compose. Technology should actively engage students as creative meaning makers who compose using multiple platforms, and we must think about how digital tools influence their writing.

INSTRUCTIONAL PRINCIPLES

Understanding how students can use technology to compose introduces additional instructional approaches. Four design principles featured in this chapter are:

1. Teaching Students to Learn with Technology. We must dismiss our assumptions that because youths have access to digital tools and technology, they are able to use technology to learn. We must provide opportunities for them to learn how to use technology to support their learning.

2. Poetry in Motion. Digital tools and platforms can be used for students to create kinetic poetry, which provides students an opportunity to remix writing while analyzing descriptive language.

3. Visual Poetry. Using tools and platforms to remix poetry can serve as an entry point for youths to create digital poetry compositions.

4. Image as Language. Students need opportunities to reflect on how technology is changing language.

In the following sections, this chapter examines four instructional approaches for digital compositions. The first section examines the complex thinking students must do when using technology. The second section focuses on kinetic poetry, which allows students to remix poetry for a deeper analysis of descriptive language. The third section delves into street photography, an instructional approach that incorporates images and writing. Finally, the chapter ends with using emojis to write, an instructional approach that highlights how images alone can be used as a form of communication, and the implications of emojis for writing. These instructional approaches and activities can help us to teach students about the power of digital tools for composing.

TEACHING STUDENTS TO LEARN WITH TECHNOLOGY

Pew Research Center (Lenhart, 2015) reports that three-quarters of young adults have access to a smartphone and that this access helps 92% of young adults to go online daily. In addition, the report reveals that texting is the prominent form of communication, with teens sending and receiving an average of 30 texts per day. While this information speaks to the types of writing youths perform daily, ubiquity of technology can lead to dangerous assumptions, as we equate using technology and digital media with knowing how to learn by using technology and digital media.

During the summer of 2014, 16 boys who were detained and considered repeat offenders (11 self-identified black, 4 self-identified white, 1 self-identified Hispanic) were surveyed about their technology use. The majority of boys attended traditional schools (75%), while 3 attended online schools, and 1 reported that he'd dropped out of school. The following data was obtained from the survey:

- 68% owned a desktop or laptop computer
- 56% had a tablet (such as an iPad)
- 87% had a smartphone
- 75% had a gaming console with online capabilities

While this is a very small number of boys surveyed, these statistics are in line with the Pew Internet report (Lenhart, 2015). However, when asked about how they used technology and the Internet, the boys reported the following:

- 37.5% used the Internet for research for school
- 68% used search engines for looking up information online
- 81% used the Internet for social media purposes
- 12% used the Internet to publish a blog
- 87% used the Internet to watch YouTube and online videos
- 87% used the Internet to watch movies
- 87% used Facebook

- 50% used Twitter
- 62.5% used Instagram

The majority of their Internet use was for social relationships and connections, not necessarily for school-related tasks. In addition, when asked how confident they felt about their abilities to use search engines to find information, only 28% responded that they were confident, 14.29% responded that they were not too confident, and 57.14% responded that they were not confident at all. None of the youths responded that they were very confident in their abilities to use search engines to find information online, even though 68% reported doing so.

This has implications for teaching youths how to use technology. We cannot assume that because they have access to technology for personal use (e.g., social media), they are confident or able to use technology for learning, problem solving, and navigating online sources. For example, youths might know how to use a program like Movie Maker to record and upload videos to YouTube, but this is different from creating a persuasive public service announcement. Youths may read information from online sources, but this does not mean that they are able to distinguish false information, recognize bias, or understand how data or statistics are used to support claims.

It is our responsibility as teachers to teach students how to critically read, analyze, and use online sources. In addition, we need to teach students how to use technology to compose. Assuming youths who are avid users of technology will automatically be skilled users and producers is problematic.

IN ACTION: AIDEN

Aiden was part of the Writing for Social Change Project described in chapter 4. As a participant in this project, Aiden was asked to select a topic he thought was important to his community and use digital media to compose in a variety of ways. Specifically, Aiden learned to write screenplays, compose public service announcements, and create TED Talks. Throughout the three-week project, he had access to a Nexus tablet for his compositions. Similar to all the young men in the Writing for Social Change Project, Aiden was part of a cognitive behavior group, meaning he was labeled as a repeat offender and was receiving additional services, such as counseling, to help him break his cycle in the juvenile court system. Aiden self-identified as white and at the time was 17 years old.

Aiden considered himself a graffiti artist and decided for his inquiry project to explore why graffiti is important in communities. With a pencil and a piece of paper, Aiden carefully sketched in bubble letters the word *discriminating*. He looked up and explained, "The word just popped in my head. Discriminating. There's a lot of people that judge others." He continued to explain that he thought people viewed graffiti artists in a negative manner and discriminated against them: "People think badly about others for expressing themselves with graffiti. But really it depends on what people write. Like, if there is a gang sign, then they think it is used to get people to join a gang. But if someone writes, like, *recycling* or something, like, important to the neighborhood, then they are like 'oh, that's cool.' I do graffiti to inspire people."

It was obvious that Aiden's identification as a graffiti artist influenced his topic choice. He also talked extensively about his brother, who was an artist. One afternoon as he was working, he shared a memory about when he was watching his brother draw a picture of Eminem and how "it looked just like him." He also explained how his brother later showed him how to draw graffiti:

> The first time I had an idea on how to draw or make graffiti is when my little brother first showed me his drawing. It was amazing. He had bubble letters above his picture, and he drew a picture of the recycling symbol and above the recycling symbol he wrote out the word *recycle* in bubble letters.

This spurred Aiden's own interest in art and solidified his admiration for his brother. Aiden explained, "I look at my brother like a role model. Like I want to be just like my little brother even though he's younger than me. He's never been to jail or nothing. That's why I look up to him."

While Aiden obviously admired his younger brother and was quick to cite him as the reason he was interested in art, he was also quick to explain their differences. Aiden described his brother as "more of an artist," while he described himself as a "graffiti artist." Aiden also explained how graffiti went from a common interest with his brother to a very important aspect of his life:

> Before I started drawing, I was always depressed or stressed out or even mad or sad. So I finally grabbed a pencil and a piece of paper and started jotting things down. I never was good at drawing until I started practicing and watched my little brother when he always drew, so I took his ideas. A couple years later, I had an idea on to draw some bubble letters out. It started to look empty so I drew a background. The background had looked empty, so I added some color to it. And now I'm creating all types of graffiti. I try different things sometimes, like different experiences. I sometimes look at different drawings and get different ideas to add to my drawings.

Aiden's love for art and desire to be a graffiti artist was the inspiration for his focus on the importance of graffiti within communities; however, the goal of the instruction was to build on Aiden's initial interest and use technology as a resource to engage him in deeper learning. Using the Nexus tablet, Aiden found evidence that graffiti could be positive within communities and composed his ideas in a variety of genres using digital tools. Aiden was not allowed to access the Internet; instead we uploaded documents for Aiden to read that offered multiple perspectives on his topic.

Aiden created a public service announcement with Movie Maker while combining multiple images of graffiti along with words to convey the importance of graffiti in communities. His argument was clear: Graffiti can be good for communities because it can inspire and encourage people in the community. He decided to immediately address one of the main criticisms of graffiti by beginning his public service announcement with a black background and the text *Graffiti is illegal unless you have permission to use the surface.*

He then created a new slide, a brick wall with a purple background and the word *Hope* written on it. He followed with an image of a black background and white text that incorporated information he learned from research: *There is strong evidence that participation in the arts can contribute to community cohesion and make people in communities feel safer and stronger* (Arts Council England, 2014). With the background of a graffiti wall and a child holding a heart-shaped balloon, he included in white font the text *Graffiti tells a story.* His composition ended with another image of graffiti, a yellow brick background with red letters reading *Believe in Yourself* and, in purple rather than white, the text *Graffiti shows a lot of emotion and inspiration.*

The images Aiden selected were powerful because they showed graffiti that contained positive messages. In particular, the picture of the child in front of the wall challenged the stereotype of graffiti and displayed its effect on all members of the community. These powerful images were accompanied by print-based words narrated by Aiden to explicitly convey his argument. Aiden used effects to smoothly transition between each slide.

Over the course of the project, Aiden's love for art influenced how he engaged with particular digital tools. Aiden would frequently use scrap paper to create pieces while in the detention center. Without access to color, Aiden's pieces were typically drawn with pencil. His favorite part about using the tablets was to create and manipulate visual images with color and other effects. For example, instead of annotating and marking up text, Aiden used PowerPoint with images of graffiti as the background. Then, when he found evidence from his readings that he thought was important, he would layer a text box onto the slide. Aiden turned an alphabetic-print act of gathering evidence into a multimodal event. In a space where he was restricted to black pencils, using the tablets gave him the space to do what he loved—think and create in color.

For Aiden, being able to remix images and use technology to create effects was powerful and engaging. Composing and using digital tools to manipulate visuals provided Aiden the opportunity to represent himself as an artist.

POETRY IN MOTION

Digital tools provide many affordances when students compose, including the opportunity to enhance meaning through additional modes. One instructional approach that uses digital tools to enhance meaning is kinetic poetry. Kinetic poetry is poetry with animated words, meaning the words move on the screen. This can be done using coding programs like Scratch or ScratchJr; however, in a classroom without access to the Internet, it is important to note that kinetic poetry can still be done with a program like PowerPoint. In PowerPoint, students can use the "Animation" tab to make words, lines, and phrases appear, disappear, move in specific paths, or change colors.

Teaching students to compose kinetic poetry is more complicated than often considered at first glance. Students have to simultaneously consider the poem's meaning and how that will be depicted and translated by words moving on the screen. Because it is not always easy to write an original poem while thinking about the words' movements, giving students many options for creating kinetic poems is important and can support students during the writing process. One instructional idea is for teachers to have published poetry or even music lyrics available to students.

After closely reading the poem or stanza, students decide which words, series of words, and lines will have movement. This is important, as the words' movement must be deliberate and purposeful to highlight a particular aspect of both the specific words and the overall meaning of the poem. In PowerPoint, students type each word or line in a separate text box so that they move in a particular way. Students then add animation to the words. For example, a word might spin, bounce on the screen, or disappear by fading out. Students can also add color, audio, or images to their slides.

Through this remixing process, students are engaged in a deeper analysis of the poem or lyrics as they consider the meaning of the movement of the words. Students must consider which words get animated, how they are animated, how all the movements will be sequenced, and the pacing. Engaging students in the process of designing kinetic poetry engages them in a sophisticated process of thinking, designing, and creating because not only must the words hold meaning as a poem, but also the visual display of the words must hold additional meaning.

IN ACTION: KINETIC POETRY

Often the writing workshops facilitated at the detention center engage students in writing for a one-hour session. During various times of the day, students come to the writing workshop classroom and work on a writing activity. Designed with my preservice teachers, this particular kinetic poetry lesson focused on having students remix poems and lyrics.

Students were given six slides featuring excerpts and lines from "Invitation" by Shel Silverstein, "Fire and Ice" by Robert Frost, "The Rose That Grew From Concrete" by Tupac, "Still I Rise" by Maya Angelou, "We Real Cool" by Gwendolyn Brooks, "Mockingbird" by Eminem, *Hamlet* by Shakespeare, and "i" by Kendrick Lamar. The purpose was to provide students with a variety of texts that could be thought-provoking and engaging.

After selecting a text, students were asked to think about how they would break the poem or lyrics into moving parts. Once they decided how to divide the text, students put words and phrases into separate text boxes and then began creating.

For example, a student named Jayden selected the slide "i" by Kendrick Lamar. The lyrics on the slide were "The sky can fall down; the wind can cry now; the strong in me; I still smile." Jayden began by thinking about the action of each stanza. For example, Jayden designed "the sky can fall down" to bounce and fall down on the screen. Jayden used this movement of the words to emphasize the word *fall*.

He then used the effects to make "the wind can cry now" move fluidly across the slide. This horizontal movement represented the wind moving. Jayden then had "the strong in me" drop letter by letter onto the screen. He explained that he wanted it to look like someone typing the line, just as someone might type a story. The last line, "I still smile" appeared in a wave motion. To finalize the slide, Jayden changed the words to a blue, scripted font. He then changed the background of the slide to gray and include a black-and-white image of bird wings.

All of these decisions brought the lyrics to life. The meaning of the lyrics no longer resided in the lyrics themselves but in the way they were visually presented and moved across the screen.

VISUAL POETRY

The saying "A picture is worth 1,000 words" captures the essence of street photography as writing. While street photography doesn't have one set definition, it is typically thought of as photography that candidly captures people in their environments. Street photos can be taken anywhere; however, many photos are taken in more urban settings. This type of photography has become more popular since 2010 with the Humans of New York project by Brandon Stanton and the 2015 book by the same name. The book documents through thousands of photographs the lives and stories of people from New York and around the world. Analyzing street photography teaches students to discern what a photo says—the story the photographer is trying to capture. Using street photography as a prompt for writing can provide students with a starting point for a story. Students have the opportunity to extend the moment captured in the photograph and write a new story about the photo. In some sense, they become the authors of a photo's story. This is an excellent strategy for teaching students about storytelling or helping students consider setting or characterization.

Many teachers use street photography as a prompt for free writing; however, when using technology like PowerPoint, street photography can be used in conjunction with found poetry to create a digital composition. Found poetry reconceptualizes words and phrases from other texts into a new poem. This is a great activity to use when students claim that they don't know what to write about, as it eases them into the writing process. There are many instructional options when combining street photography and found poetry.

First Option: Using PowerPoint, a teacher provides students with a preselected image and a list of words to use as the basis for an original poem. The students use the image as the background of the slide and then layer and arrange the words on the slide to create a new poem.

Second Option: As a whole class, a teacher and students select one image they think is interesting. Together, they brainstorm words that describe the image and use these words as a basis for a poem. Again, students use the image as the background of the slide and then layer and arrange the words on the slide to create a new poem.

Third Option: A teacher provides students with preselected images to choose from and PowerPoint slides containing three to four poems with descriptive language. Students read the poems and highlight or underline the words that are descriptive or interesting. After reviewing their words, students select the photo that they think fits their word selection. They then use the words to write an original poem that corresponds to the photo. Students arrange the image and words on the slide to create a new poem.

Using a digital tool like PowerPoint allows students to arrange the image and words to convey meaning. The result is a visual composition in which words and image work together to create meaning.

IN ACTION: AUDRE

I first met Audre while he was on probation and attending a weekly writing group. Each week he dressed impeccably, in all the latest fashion with brand-name labels, especially Sean John and Rocawear. He described himself as creative but didn't think of himself as an artist.

After three weeks on probation, Audre was arrested and placed back at the detention center, where he was in and out over the next six months. During his time in the center, Audre attended the weekly writing workshops. One evening, the intersection of street photography and writing seemed particularly interesting to him. While Audre was typically an active participant, the street photography lesson really stimulated powerful writing ideas.

Audre had access to a folder of images on a Nexus tablet that he was allowed to use during the workshop. After browsing through the images, he selected a photo of a girl covered in mud. The only color besides the brown mud smeared on her face was her startling blue eyes. He later explained that he thought the photo "looked interesting" because of the contrast between the mud and the girl's very blue eyes.

On three PowerPoint slides, Audre had poems by e. e. cummings ("87," "If I," and "53"). After reading the poems, Audre used the highlighting tool for words he thought were descriptive and interesting. From these words, Audre created the original found poem at the beginning of this chapter.

Then, still using PowerPoint, he layered the words on the image to highlight the emotion of the photo and the words. Using a digital tool provided him the opportunity to engage in the sophisticated process of remixing content—e. e. cummings's poems and the image—to create a new multimodal poem.

IMAGE AS LANGUAGE

In a popular TED Talk, John McWhorter (2013) dismissed the notion that text messaging is killing the English language. Recognizing that many people view the replacement of traditional English with text language as a deficit, he argues that technology is instead linguistically shifting language. Students become dual-language users as they shift back and forth from text language to standardized English. According to McWhorter (2013), this is an asset and strength rather than a deficit.

Similarly, Turner and colleagues (2014) coined the term *digitalk* to encompass the language adolescents use in digital platforms. Their research demonstrates that students who go back and forth between traditional English and text speak develop "metalinguistic awareness" (p. 29); they are able to think critically about linguistics and the appropriateness of varying forms of language.

McWhorter's (2013) TED Talk and Turner and colleagues' (2014) research demonstrate the importance of recognizing and valuing the ways youth linguistically develop as writers. Technology continues to shape our written and spoken language. Text speak is no longer only abbreviations (e.g., LOL and OMG) but now also includes emojis as visual representations of words. (Many smartphones now even replace words with emojis.) This means students must be strategic readers of visuals in order to fully understand written messages.

IN ACTION: EMOJIS TO COMPOSE

A one-hour writing workshop session at the detention center was devoted to students exploring the relationship between emojis and language. The goal of the lesson was to demonstrate emojis' meanings and how we use them in our social and cultural written texts. This also provided a critical interpretation of emojis and how we use these visuals to represent ideas and emotions.

Students each had access to a Nexus tablet with a PowerPoint slide. On each slide was a line from a canonical piece of literature. For example, "A single man in possession of a good fortune must be in want of a wife" (Austen, *Pride and Prejudice*) and "They wanted to speak, but could not, tears stood in their eyes" (Dostoevsky, *Crime and Punishment*). Students then used emojis to replace each word with a visual. Finally, they shared their translated lines and discussed how they used the same and different emojis for particular words. This led to larger conversations about which images best represent which words and why.

This lesson introduced students to emoji writing as they wrote original texts composed only with emojis. For example, John wrote, "I can't wait to get out" using the emojis of a man, eyes, a calendar, and a man running. Sam wrote, "If you don't have love, you don't have happiness" and used a man, a no-entry image, a heart, and a face with a tear. While the youths proclaimed this as a fun activity, the critical framing allowed a deeper conversation into language and how we use language in culturally and socially appropriate ways.

CONCLUSION

Focusing on language as a "multimodal event" (Harste, Woodward, & Burke, 1984) affords us the opportunity to reconceptualize our notions about what writing really is and what counts as writing. We can shift away from the dominant view of literacy as traditional print reading and writing to a broader literacy that encompasses many modes of communication. Technology can advance our notions of what it means to compose. For example, written alphabetic text can be positioned as secondary to meaning making when we consider how students use digital tools for the purposeful arrangement of words to depict movement or how a photo can communicate emotion.

Digital compositions highlight the recursive relationship between writing and technology. Technology continues to help people produce new modes, genres, and ways to communicate, continually influencing how people define writing. For example, tweets, blogs, and posts are new genres of communication. Our desire to communicate has also shaped new technologies. And yet, in schools we tend to hold onto narrow definitions of writing that lead us to overlook the sophisticated compositions that people engage in every day. Scrolling through an adolescent's Instagram account or a teacher's Pinterest board or a librarian's YouTube account reveals fitting examples of how visual and audio modes are vital to the ways we demonstrate our knowledge and communicate with the world.

Bringing digital tools into the classroom allows for critical examinations of how people communicate effectively and how our means of communication are constantly shifting (Mills, 2009). Traditionally, we think of writing as having conventions and rules that one must follow; however, new technologies have shaped what it means to write and communicate, what is considered appropriate, and which conventions direct writing practices.

Involving students with digital tools and technology at the detention center is important work. Students at the center love using technology because technology is the unfamiliar familiar; they use technology in their daily lives, yet they don't often have opportunities to learn with technology. They are consumers of technology, often using digital tools to maintain social relationships. They know how to use social media sites, watch videos on YouTube, and play online video games. They don't, however, often have opportunities to be creators, designers, and innovators. Therefore, while they may be familiar with technology, they can experience digital tools in a new way—as producers of writing.

While detained, youths do not typically have access to technology. If they do have access, they are often using prescriptive programs focused on basic skill acquisition. And yet, outside of the detention center, most youths receive information about the world through online sources. We want all students to be skilled at searching for information using digital tools and deciphering online sources when engaged in complex reading tasks. Furthermore, we want students to be positioned as both consumers and producers of digital media and compositions. While we must recognize the security measures that many detention centers are federally mandated to follow, we need to work strategically with detention centers so youths have access to technology. When we deny them the knowledge of how to use a digital tool for learning, we are not simply denying them a tool; we are denying them learning.

Chapter Six

Risky Endeavors

The overarching purpose of this book is to urge educators to adapt research-based writing instruction to meet the needs of all learners in all learning spaces. This requires us to acknowledge and value students' personal writing practices while understanding what their stories mean for our instruction. We also need to ask students to write about social issues that are important in their lives and communities by teaching evidence-based writing as a way to connect them to their communities and broaden their knowledge of the world. And finally, we must advocate for students to have access to technology so they can learn with and use digital media for the composing process.

As we move forward, we must consider the broader implications for these instructional approaches and how we educate youths. There are four fundamental instructional implications for educators committed to all the youths they teach or come into contact with on a daily basis. In addition to these instructional implications, there are research and policy implications that deserve our attention. This chapter explores implications for instruction, research, and policies.

These implications are not only applicable to those teaching or researching in juvenile detention centers or prisons. These are implications that can be broadly considered for all schools and areas where we work with youths.

INSTRUCTIONAL IMPLICATIONS

We must value youths' personal writing and broaden our ideas about what counts as writing. As teachers we need to know our students as writers. This goes beyond labeling them as writers to knowing what they write and why. Knowing a person's writing practices (what they write, why they write)

"We'll be O.k"

Sometimes I sit at night, wondering
what more I can do.
Since I'm gonna be your mom, I have
to do whats best for you.
I often apologize, for things I've
Said or done.
Baby just know in my heart, you'll
always be number one.
I know daddies not around right now
but we'll be OK.
Because daddie dont think twice, about
who he hurts or betrays.
Daddy knows what he's done, yet he
Still dont care.
My baby I'm sorry, In the end he
Probably wont be there.
Baby I'm here, And we'll always
get through strong.
Even IF daddy, wont right his
Wrongs.
So follow me baby, and I'll
Show you the way.
I'm still here, we'll be Ok.
Just know momies still here.
watching out for you.
Pg. 1

Neveah's poem to her unborn baby

informs who they are, what they believe, how they spend their time, and what they value.

Sometimes it is very easy to get to know students as writers. Often at the detention center, young adults express how much they enjoy writing without prompting. They freely discuss what and why they write. They immediately identify themselves as writers. If asked if they are writers, the majority of students initially respond with a resounding no. But scroll their phones, and hundreds of text messages and social media posts appear. Their notebooks contain poems, raps, and stories. By digging and searching, we can discover the tremendous amount of writing that students perform on a daily basis.

The disconnect between what adolescents are doing (writing) and what they *think* they are doing (not really writing) seems to happen because of their perception of what counts as writing and subsequently who counts as writers. Many adolescents view writing as a five-paragraph essay or a literary analysis in response to reading literature. Writing in this sense becomes oppressive, something that only happens in schools, something that is assigned, something that is done to them, not something they choose to do.

Society and educators predominantly hold preconceived notions of *what counts as writing*. Too often a literary analysis is considered writing, while social media use is not; a five-paragraph argumentative essay using textual evidence is thought to be more rigorous than a work of poetry. And unfortunately, this is often reinforced in schools, on educational assessments, and in our current educational policies. The Common Core State Standards (CCSS) guiding many states' curriculum and instruction have divided writing instruction into three genres: narrative, informative, and argumentative. This often guides teachers' instruction, so writing is taught as silos in which students learn to write one genre at a time instead of learning how genres inform one another and how authors use multiple genres in their writing. In addition, standardized assessments categorize writing as short answers, extended responses, and essays. This is not the type of writing adolescents read or write in their daily lives, and standardized assessments reinforce that writing is done at or for only school purposes. And yet, the National Council of Teachers of English's (NCTE) policy report states that "writing grows out of many purposes."

When literacy is viewed as a one-dimensional activity on a standardized assessment, the rich and important ways adolescents engage in writing is overlooked. If we broaden what counts as writing, then the definition of who is a writer is likewise broadened. This perspective implies that teachers should not only recognize the ways adolescents write but should also consider *why* adolescents write. This consideration highlights the question, What purposes does writing serve adolescents? Looking closely at and valuing the writing adolescents do for pleasure acknowledges the importance of writing in the lives of adolescents, and encourages student to write and view themselves as writers.

The question is changed from, What is the value of adolescents' writing in relationship to school-sanctioned writing? to *What is the value of writing in relationship to adolescents' lives?* And thus, a different perspective emerges that all adolescents are writers.

IN ACTION: AIDEN'S POETRY

Aiden, featured in chapter 5, sat down, folded his hands in front of him, and prepared to be interviewed about his experiences designing a public service announcement and writing a TED Talk based on the role of graffiti in communities. Over the three-week period of working with Aiden, he consistently shared how much he likes to write, so we began our conversation by talking about what he writes and why:

> Aiden: I just like to write poetry for my girl. Mostly because she just wants me to write it for her. And I'm just really good at it, so I just write it for her.
>
> Kristine: You don't have to, but do you want to tell me more about that?
>
> Aiden: I usually write about how I'm in love with her or whatever. That's mostly it. Me and her.
>
> Kristine: And do you send her your poems while you are here?
>
> Aiden: Yes, I send it through letters. Like, I just write down all my feelings in poetry. Like this is how I feel and I really miss you. Whatever. And I put it in the mailbags to send to her.
>
> Kristine: Do you write her poetry when you aren't in the detention center?
>
> Aiden: Oh yeah. But I don't send it. I put it on Facebook. She really likes that. Girls like poetry. And other people, especially her friends, will read it and respond with a like or comment such as "Aaawwwww." She likes that.

Aiden continued to explain that poetry is a way to communicate to his girlfriend his feelings, but he also writes poetry when he is "mad or angry or really sad." He explained:

It just helps me. It's like you can only hold so much in. It's like a two-liter. If you hold so much of your feelings in, you just blow up. You explode. You gotta figure out a way to get it out. I write poetry. That gets it out.

THE MYTH OF THE STRUGGLING WRITER

How writing is defined can extend to the perceptions of students as writers. When the writing adolescents do in school is counted as the *only* writing, then students are known in only one way. This is problematic for teaching students who are viewed as struggling, marginalized, or disenfranchised. By focusing on the type of writing students produce in school, teachers only know them as struggling, marginalized, or disenfranchised. Adolescents who struggle to meet the norms of society are viewed as deficient, behind their peers, and in need of remediation. As a consequence, educators fail to see them as writers and the many ways they engage in writing.

Youths in detention centers are often viewed as struggling learners, specifically with reading and writing, as numerous studies indicate that detained and incarcerated youths are often years behind their peers in reading levels. In addition, there is an overrepresentation in juvenile detention centers and prisons of youths who need special education services. Much of this research examines students' academic abilities measured by standardized assessments, but these studies fail to acknowledge the many ways that adolescents engage in meaningful reading and writing practices.

It is unwise and inaccurate to only view students as either *writers* or *nonwriters*. This is deficit thinking, because the focus is on students' weaknesses rather than their strengths. While this means that teachers must take responsibility for their assumptions about adolescents, researchers also warn that we cannot dismiss what Nieto and Bode (2008) call the sociopolitical context of schooling: "the unexamined ideologies and myths that shape commonly accepted ideas and values in a society" (p. 7).

Unfortunately, we often have preconceived notions of the term *struggling writer* and the kids to whom we've assigned this label. We may think of struggling writers as those who have difficulties with grammar and mechanics or with constructing complex sentences. Or we may think of struggling writers as those students whom we consider reluctant to write, an attitude that masks their capabilities. This mislabels students because there is no such thing as a struggling writer. Every writer working to achieve a goal is, at some point during the writing process, a struggling writer. When we use fixed labels, such as *proficient* or *struggling*, we create a division—those who *are* writers and those who *are not*. Yet, these are false categories. And as teachers, we are responsible for breaking down this dichotomy. There are only writers. And our classrooms are filled with them.

It is our goal as teachers to see all students as writers, and that is very much the goal of this book—to recognize the complex ways youths write in their personal lives and to highlight how ambitious instruction and encouragement can engage students who have been forgotten, ignored, marginalized, and disenfranchised.

The 2016 NCTE policy report explicitly states, "[E]veryone has the capacity to write; writing can be taught; and teachers can help students become better writers." This fundamental belief shapes our view that all students in our classrooms are writers, and we as teachers are committed to supporting their growth and development. While this seems like common sense, this belief is not always enacted in schools and classrooms, particularly when we label our students as struggling writers.

We must deconstruct the notions of proficient and struggling writers and instead view all students as writers working toward their own writing goals, who with instruction and support can continue to achieve these goals. It is our responsibility to reach even the students who *seem* most reluctant and most disengaged so they can uncover their own purposes for writing and see writing as something they can achieve in their academic lives.

IN ACTION: SAM

It was a Wednesday, which at the detention center meant that students could go to the library to check out books to take to their cells. Sam was 13, a small black boy in a room full of teenagers twice his size. He sat at his table intently studying a "how to draw" book in front of him, open to a two-page layout about how to draw a crocodile.

A preservice teacher who was doing his field experience at the detention center was teaching. Because it was the week of Halloween, the teacher decided on a lesson on writing scary stories. As the lesson began, Sam was still looking at the crocodile images, his brow furrowed. The other students were beginning to write, some collaborating on a story.

Allie, another preservice teacher, made her way to Sam's table and sat beside him. He gave her a shy, sideways smile, like he knew she was going to ask him if he wanted to write. "Why did you pick out this book?" she asked. He smiled, shrugged, and said, "I want to learn to draw. And these crocodiles look mean." "Hmmm. Why do you think they look mean?" she asked. He studied the book and pointed. "See these teeth? See? You have to draw them real pointy. Like they are really sharp." "They do look pointy sharp, scary sharp. Maybe our story can be about a crocodile," she said. He smiled, knowing he was right all along. Allie's next question was what he guessed she would ask when she first sat down: "Do you want to write together?"

Maybe he was lonely. Most likely he thought that saying no to Allie would get him into trouble. Or maybe because he just felt like saying yes. For whatever reason, he agreed, and they took turns crafting a story about a crocodile living in a public pool. People became victims as the crocodile chomped off limbs. While writing, Sam stopped to ask about punctuation: "Should I use a comma?" Or they discussed literary devices: "Chomp, chomp, chomp," he said, smiling at his ferocious crocodile. Allie asked if he knew the term for a word that has a sound associated with it. He was unsure, and when Allie told him, he nodded. They continued their collaborative writing exercise. Throughout the writing, he asked questions about when to use commas or periods and when certain words should be capitalized. By the end of the writing period, they had crafted a complete scary story to share with the class.

After the session, Allie reflected on her experience working with Sam:

> At first, when we started working together, I thought he was really going to have trouble with the assignment. At first, he didn't seem like he really wanted to participate, but then when he realized he could write about something he was already interested in, then he was more willing. I think topic choice was really motivating.

Reflecting on their collaborative writing, she noted, "He had ideas. He knew what he wanted to write about. I was able to support him by helping him articulate some of the things he wanted to say, but with just a little guidance and feedback, he was able to write his creative story."

Provide Ambitious Writing Instruction

Our writing instruction must match the rich ways youths engage in writing. As writing teachers we must recognize and value our students' personal writing practices, while acknowledging that reading and writing can be dignifying tools. Writing can help students to locate themselves when they feel lost, to reconstruct their stories, and to express themselves. However, we must also design writing instruction that builds on their experiences while broadening their worlds and knowledge of writing (Moje, 2000). For example, youths need opportunities to challenge the dominant narratives of their lives by creating countertexts or counternarratives to represent the multiple ways they make themselves known to the world. They need opportunities to engage in argumentative and persuasive writing that requires them to gather evidence, make sense of evidence, and use evidence to support their opinions. And they need writing instruction that allows them to both critique their marginalization and create ways for them to take actions for a more equitable society. This requires ample time devoted to writing as a creative, meaning-making activity; opportunities to write daily; and many reasons to write.

Research demonstrates that unless students are in advanced placement classes or attending International Baccalaureate schools, many students do not receive writing instruction outside writing for standardized tests (Applebee & Langer, 2012). And yet, all students deserve rich and ambitious writing instruction. Langer (2002) uses the term *high literacy* experiences—the "deeper knowledge of the ways in which reading, writing, language, and content work together" (p. 3). All youths, particularly those we've pushed to remedial courses or who are detained, do not need poor writing experiences in the form of worksheets about grammar or constructing complex sentences. They do not need an overemphasis on strategies that reinforce writing as a skills-based endeavor. All youths need writing instruction that develops their writing knowledge and supports them in achieving their writing goals.

Write in a Variety of Genres

Students need opportunities to study writing and engage in a variety of substantial acts of writing. In many high school English classrooms, longer pieces of writing are focused on literary analysis about a great piece of literature, but it is important that students have opportunities to write authentic genres. For example, students should craft argumentative or persuasive types of writing, such as TED Talks, public service announcements, and blogs. They should also have time to compose narrative pieces, such as poetry and flash fiction. We want students to see the types of writing that exist and realize that they can be authors of those texts.

Use Rhetorical Knowledge

Writing instruction should build students' rhetorical knowledge: their knowledge of text structure, audience, and the social context or purpose of writing. We want students to recognize that writing has a social purpose, that we write for a particular reason and for a particular audience. It is easier for students to craft a piece of writing when they understand why they are writing the piece and who will be reading their work. This information drives the decisions they make as authors.

Apply Strategic Knowledge

Students should have a wide range of strategies to guide their writing and make decisions about their knowledge. Writing is a complex process, and when students have knowledge of strategy, they are better equipped to plan, draft, and revise their writing. Teacher modeling is an effective way to guide students throughout the writing process. Teachers should think aloud through their own writing to help students see how authors make decisions when writing and to see how others use strategies to help them through the writing process.

Be Able to Use Technology and Digital Tools

Technology is ubiquitous. In order to be truly literate, students must know how to compose with digital tools or within digital spaces and online platforms. If we don't provide students opportunities to learn by using technology, then we are denying them the tools they need to learn, work, and live in the 21st century. Furthermore, technology is constantly changing. We cannot teach students certain platforms or digital tools. Instead, we must teach students how to learn with technology and to use digital tools to think critically and creatively solve problems.

Use Critical Literacy

Students need to use literacy as a way to make meaning of their lives and voice their opinions. Reading and writing should not be viewed as only functional skills, but rather students need to understand how to decipher complex texts, recognize bias, and uncover multiple interpretations of texts.

In addition, we want to help students view writing as a cultural practice that can propel them to be civically involved. Morrell (2008) writes, "[S]tudents still need to understand the mechanics and use of language"; however, he notes, "[W]ithin a critical theory of writing instruction, even those texts that emerge from the classroom have a purpose and audience much larger than the teacher or the classroom: students produce texts that can change the world" (p. 86). We want students to be empowered to question and critique so they can participate in broader conversations about their communities and the world. This type of instruction will help them to challenge the inequitable circumstances they may face in school, in their community, and in society.

IN ACTION: TYREE'S CONCRETE POETRY

Tyree, a 17-year-old self-identified black male, cycled in and out of the detention center, which also meant that he cycled in and out of the weekly writing workshop at the detention center. When he attended the writing workshop, he often wrote extensively for the entire hour. He was quiet and reserved during the writing workshop.

His demeanor was different the night we composed concrete poetry. Concrete, or visual, poetry is not only conveyed through words but also through how the words are visually represented. In concrete poetry, the words are arranged in a manner that depicts the subject or theme of the poem. This requires students to understand how image and text can be combined in order to create meaning. Students simultaneously consider the poem's meaning and translate that into an image depicted by rearranging the words.

On this night, Tyree was particularly motivated. He wanted to not only share his writing but also explain to the group why he created his visual poem the way he did. To facilitate students' learning, we first read and analyzed concrete poems. Afterward, they were given two options for creating their concrete poem. The first option was to reformat an already-published poem into a concrete poem. The poems were selections from Tupac's (2009) book of poetry *The Rose That Grew from Concrete*, including "If There Be Pain," "And 2morrow," and "The Rose That Grew from Concrete." The second option was to write an original piece and create the arrangement of words.

Tyree chose the second option. He immediately had a sense of the image he wanted to depict and began writing and visually creating simultaneously. Using the image of interlocking lines of text, he explained his poem visually represented a fence or bars, with the idea that people are fenced into the juvenile justice system. Tyree initially used only words, just as the model poems did; however, at the end he also created a copy that included lines around the words to emphasize that the bars.

The first lines of the poem used the word *some* in horizontal lines to represent the youths and their varying stories of being detained. He then switched and used the words *same* in vertical lines. Tyree explained that he wanted to show that while everyone has a unique experience, there are often commonalities and shared stories that make them the same.

Tyree's words are a powerful testament to youths' experiences in the detention center. They tend to be transient in nature. The detention center, for some, can serve as a short-term placement while they are waiting for trial, and therefore, they may be there for as short as 24 hours. There are also youths at the center for months, waiting for trials and court sentences. Many are at the detention center for a month, gone for a month, and then back again. They spend their adolescence cycling through the juvenile justice system. Tyree's poem voices the repetitiveness of this cycle.

While his words create a strong message, the combination of the image and words create a powerful statement. The horizontal and vertical lines are a visual representation of youths' inability to escape the cycle and the system. They literally see bars every day, and their stories in bars represent their time in the detention center. Tyree's poem exemplifies how composing with image can engage youths in sophisticated acts of critical and creative meaning making. Tyree built on his experiences to call readers' attention to the oppressive cycle of the juvenile justice system.

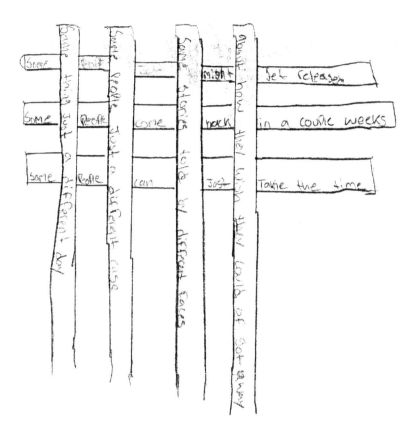

Tyree's concrete poem

BEING DISCERNING EDUCATORS

Writing instruction in juvenile detention facilities is complicated work. As educators we must recognize the complexity of teaching students who are detained. We must be discerning instructors, thoughtfully designing each lesson plan and activity. Hinshaw and Jacobi (2015) reminds those who conduct writing programs in prisons that while providing incarcerated people with a voice, we must recognize that we are working in an institution built on confinement and control. Hinshaw and Jacobi (2015) argue,

> We must acknowledge the limits and compromises necessary in any carceral education program; however noble the aims and values of our educational programs, they seldom literally "break down the walls," despite the romanticized ways by which we might like to talk about them or the titles we might use for our published collections. This is also about understanding the extent to

Same ~thing~ Just a different day/
Same People Just a different case
Same Storing/How told by different They faces could have got away
about

Words from Tyree's concrete poem

> which our participation in prison programs makes us complicit in the larger prison-industrial complex; working to improve the conditions of women's incarceration is not the same as, and may in fact be in direct opposition to, working to abolish the modern prison system.

We must be thoughtful about our instructional approaches. For example, writing teachers often promote the use of author chairs to invite students to share their writing. This is built on the idea that there is power in having an authentic audience and writing is strengthened through talking and sharing. While this may be true, teachers need to exercise discretion with instruction. Having students read their work aloud can be powerful; however, this can position students in a dangerous space when detained. Guards are listening. Cameras are recording. Other youths may be judging. Teachers must negotiate a complex learning space and be aware of the ways students are represented through their writing. We must also recognize how our actions contribute, both positively and negatively, to students' positioning.

IN ACTION: "IT'S MY PRIDE"

The transient nature of the detention centers requires teachers to be flexible and organized. Amanda (chapter 4) and I use manila folders to organize

Tyree's poem without the bars

students' writing. However, for the youths, the manila folders became sites for complex and meaningful literacy practices. Unprompted, they began to draw and write on their folders. After a few days of watching them studiously sketching on the folders, I asked Patrick (in chapter 2), a student, why he did this. He responded, "When you [Kristine] pass them out, people will be like this [holding up the folder to show others]. Everyone sees it [what he drew and wrote], and it's important. It's my pride."

While we viewed the folders as simple way for youths to keep their writing, they used the folders to display their identities (Pytash, 2014). In a space where youths are stripped of the markers that they use to outwardly identify themselves (e.g., dress, hair, makeup), the folders and their literacy practices served this purpose. When I asked Patrick privately about his folder, he immediately pointed out the quote that he credited himself for writing: "Don't live with your head in the clouds." He explained, "I made it up. But it makes sense. 'Cause, like, if you're living with your head in the clouds, you know, you're not thinking straight. You're not looking forward, not focusing."

He continued to explain other images and words on his folder. He commented that his gang kept him focused on things that are important, like their motto "Death b4 Dishonor," taken from a song. He explained that Air Force 1s are his favorite shoes, and he also included references to his city. He also had erased a six-point star that he drew. When I asked why, he explained that he carved the same star on his wall in his cell, and he was afraid someone might see it, and he would get in trouble. He said, "I am supposed to go to a place, like a home, after I leave here, but if I get in trouble in here, it gets revoked, and then what if I go to prison?"

When I asked why he drew anything, he explained, "'Cause that's who I am. All this stuff on here is who I am. I did it for me. But I am good at drawing, so I wanted people to see my masterpiece." He continued,

> You don't have to tell people who you are, like you don't have to put it straight out there. You can make people think about what's on your folder. Like, you don't wanna say, "Well, I'm this, I'm that." But putting it on your folder where everyone can see it, well, then people gotta think about it. And they might find out what it means, but they might not.

RESEARCH IMPLICATIONS

We must consider what pedagogy means for research as we work to advance knowledge of effective writing instruction. Scholars have been advocating for teacher research for decades (Cochran-Smith & Lytle, 1993), particularly how teachers document the instructional practices and the resulting student learning in their classrooms.

The field needs to examine the pedagogical practices most effective in developing students as readers and writers. For example, as technology redefines our ideas about composing, we need additional research on the students' process when writing with digital tools. We also need research on how students engage in literacy.

In addition to investigating students' academic abilities, we need to research students' writing dispositions. Many youths in juvenile detention centers have had unsuccessful school experiences and do not always have positive views of themselves as learners. Teachers must investigate various types of instruction that influence youths' dispositions as well as their academic engagement and motivation.

Furthermore, a worthwhile area of research is how innovative learning environments influence detained youths' abilities and perceptions of themselves as learners. Teachers can examine how technology in alternative learning environments may advance educational opportunities for youths. Not only does researching pedagogy allow teachers to claim ownership over their professional development, but also this research can be valuable for understanding current educational trends.

In addition to disseminating research on instructional practices, teachers should document the methodologies they use to investigate teaching and learning. Not only do we need to better understand the tools teachers use to examine and document their teaching, but we also need to advance the field's understanding of alternative research methods that can provide crucial perspectives on teaching and learning.

Positioning youths as researchers is also paramount. Youth Participatory Action Research (YPAR) is one such methodology that includes students as researchers involved in critical inquiries. This methodology allows youths to identify ways to improve their lives and their communities (Fine et al., 2007; Morrell, 2008). Furthermore, we could explore the ways youth, even when detained, can make research contributions to their learning in the many spaces where they are educated.

Teachers and students can disseminate their research through their networks in their schools, districts, and professional organizations. In addition, social media provides platforms that allow teachers to have a global audience. This is crucial; teacher and student researchers are valuable for informing educational practices, research, and policies.

POLICIES FOR A MORE EQUITABLE EDUCATION

Research has demonstrated that high-literacy classrooms with substantial acts of reading and writing typically occur in advanced placement classrooms or in schools with specialized programming (Applebee & Langer, 2011). Educational policies are needed to ensure that all students have access to the learning opportunities afforded in high-literacy classrooms. As advocates for our students, we must argue that these policies are not driven solely by the performance of students on top-down standardized assessments that often result in confining writing instruction to test preparation. We need educational policies that do more than measure student growth on test scores and reinforce the idea that literacy is merely a skill.

Policies that recognize the complexity of learning and provide adequate support for all students to develop as readers and writers are crucial. Policies drive the decisions made in schools, and the current climate is one of labeling and pushing students out of schools, often contributing to the criminalization of our most marginalized and victimized adolescents.

When we label youths, we discursively position them, meaning we assign words to them that we know are not neutral and evoke feelings, attitudes, and memories. These labels in turn become the stories we construct about the students in our classroom, and those stories make up their identities. Labeling students result in educational policies that physically position students. For example, when students are "bad," we move them to rooms in schools for in-school suspension. We police students in hallways until we are able to push them out of school and into alternative schools. We move them to such places as juvenile detention facilities. It is no secret that we use labels to create the policies that push certain students out of our schools.

We label and push out students based on race. Black students are 3.5 times more likely than their white classmates to be suspended or expelled. Studies on the relationships between students' racial identities, their behavior, and suspension have found that even while black students are not misbehaving more frequently, they are suspended at higher rates. In addition, young black men are arrested, charged, and receive harsher sentences than any other population of youths (Brinkley-Rubinstein, Craven, & McCormack, 2014; Leiber & Fox, 2005; Noguera, 2003).

We label and push out students based on gender. As a society, the stereotype of girls is that they are supposed to be "nice, to be a joy to their parents and an example of correctness in the way they act" (Chesney-Lind & Sheldon, 2004, p. xi). Chesney-Lind and Sheldon (2004) argue that girls' involvement in the juvenile justice system is on the rise because their behavior does not fit the stereotype. Research show that girls involved in the juvenile justice system tend to be physically and sexually abused. These traumatic experiences often result in their involvement in the juvenile court system, and their experiences within the system are influenced by their gender.

We label and push out students based on economic circumstances. Being a child of poverty increases one's risk of entering the juvenile justice system (Vidal et al., 2017).

We label and push out students based on emotional and mental health. Students with emotional and mental health disorders are more likely to struggle academically and may drop out of school. In addition, research demonstrates 70% of young adults within the juvenile justice system have a mental health diagnosis (Scott, Underwood, & Lamis, 2015).

In comparison to labels attached to students' race, gender, socioeconomic status, and emotional and mental health, labels of being a proficient or struggling writer might seem inconsequential. And yet, we know that labels prescribe students certain types of instructional experiences. Students who are "smart" and behaviorally "good" take advanced placement courses and succeed academically. Students who are not perceived as smart or who act out take remedial courses. These labels determine the experiences they will have in schools. Labels are powerful. And when we attach educational policies to them, labels are dangerous.

Teachers may read this book and think, "These aren't the students I teach." And yet, too often when we discuss issues of equity within schools, we focus on what happens in traditional school settings and classrooms. We ignore that youths are often educated in community-based settings, after-school programs, virtual schools, alternative schools, juvenile detention centers, and prisons. As teachers, scholars, researchers, and policy makers, we must attend to the environments where kids are educated because an ideal like equity cannot happen until we recognize the many spaces where kids are educated.

We need educational policies that assist teachers and scholars in traversing contested learning spaces, such as juvenile detention centers, and navigating the associated tension. If we overlook or simply criticize these spaces as contested without acting, then we also disenfranchise and marginalize youths. When we ignore these spaces, we ignore the voices of youths living through the trauma of confinement and incarceration. We ignore the educational needs of these students.

We cannot challenge the current deficit narrative of youths—those most marginalized and disenfranchised—if we refuse to acknowledge the spaces where they are educated. We need more research that uncovers and explores emerging patterns of inequities in classrooms. Finally, we need educational policies that do not criminalize and marginalize youth by labeling and pushing them out of school but instead incorporate nonpunitive restorative approaches for students who need our support.

IN ACTION: NEVEAH

I first met Neveah (featured in the introduction) when she was 12 and attending a jail-based alternative school because she was constantly truant. She had been in and out of foster homes and suffered maltreatment, including abuse and neglect. She was white, living in poverty, and pregnant by 13.

At the beginning of her pregnancy, she returned to live with her mother, four sisters, and one brother. One morning my phone rang at 3:00 a.m., and Neveah—always a soft talker—whispered, "Kristy, I just want you to know that I am not going to school today." The quiet of her voice was almost completely drowned out by the noise in the background, including someone yelling, "Who are you talking to?" Quickly, in a hushed voice, she said, "I'm okay, just tired. So I am not going to school," and then she hung up.

We saw each other a few days later, and she explained that she typically doesn't get much sleep at home. Her excuse was that "something is always going on." She continued, "My sister had a baby, so I am taking care of her baby and my brother's baby. He doesn't even know if he is the father, but the mom doesn't take care of the baby, so I have to." Neveah, pregnant with her first child, also functioned as the main childcare provider of two babies. And yet, each time we met, her journal was filled with poems. Even with the chaos of her life, she made time to write poetry.

Despite being a prolific writer, school was never a place Neveah would be successful. Class after class, she opened up her notebook and then put her head down. She didn't bother participating in class, and no one bothered to ask her to participate. Not one teacher came by her desk to offer a word of encouragement, to ask her questions, or even to reprimand her for not doing her work. Neveah was invisible.

Her teachers certainly didn't pay attention to the fact that she always carried a personal writing journal filled with poetry or that sometimes she had worn books from the school library open on her desk. Instead, this is what they noticed:

Teacher 1: She is going to start showing, and that isn't something I want my daughter to see. I don't want my child to know she has a classmate who is pregnant. I don't want her to see that.

Teacher 2: She never makes up any of her homework. I don't know what she does at home, but it isn't her homework. I am going to have to give her an incomplete or an F.

Teacher 3: I can't understand why she doesn't just do homeschooling.

Rather than showing her compassion, her teachers displayed anger, resentment, and indifference. Her pregnant belly made them uncomfortable. The chaos of her life overwhelmed them. Her presence was a nuisance.

Neveah is purposefully featured at the beginning and end of this book because she isn't the exception; she is the norm. She is an adolescent who seems too young to have endured such painful life experiences, an adolescent who has been manipulated, used, and disregarded by the social systems meant to support, nurture, and educate her. She pursues writing as a way to make sense of her life, express her feelings, and learn about the world. And yet, she is so disengaged in this nonresponsive environment that she doesn't mind being pushed out of school. In fact, leaving school seems like a better option than making the effort to attend school.

Her teachers made it very clear that Neveah's poverty and her pregnancy made her a "bad" girl, a youth "undeserving" of an education. Months after her early-morning phone call, she e-mailed me from school to tell me that she was going to try attending a virtual school run by the state. She thought that would be better for her education because she could care for her baby and her sister's and brother's babies while attending this virtual school.

Neveah gave birth to a little girl and tried to attend the virtual school but soon found attending classes online more difficult than she originally imagined. She once again found herself truant, and once again she found herself relegated to attending the alternative school and later the juvenile detention center. This cycle—the one that *we* pushed Neveah into—eventually led her to the juvenile court system, a place that once youths enter they very rarely leave.

FINAL THOUGHTS

McAdams (1993) writes that people are "all tellers of tales, and we seek to provide our scattered and often confusing experiences with a sense of coherence by arranging the episodes of our lives" (p. 11). For young adults, writing about their experiences provides them a way to make sense of their worlds, serving as a counter for the narratives that dominate their lives and a way to voice what they cannot speak. Writing allows young adults to tell their tales, and this book shares the tales of those young people whose voices are often forgotten and pushed to the margins of our society.

Winn (2011) writes, "[I]ncarcerated children should be a signal to adults that there is work to do and that youth need opportunities to be heard" (p. 143). Teachers must take up this work. This may seem risky as we calculate the immense responsibility and unique privilege we have when teaching students how to cultivate their writing—their tales. However, writing teachers must be willing to do this work. We must appreciate when our students write to examine the episodes of their lives, while teaching them ways to critically and analytically make sense of their worlds through writing. We must incorporate research-based instructional practices that emphasize writing as a social and cultural practice so that we nurture the writers in our classrooms, while empowering them to question, critique, and produce the narratives that will create a more equitable society. Finally, we must consistently reflect on and question our pedagogical practices to make sure we are not undermining youths' many forms of written expression and reinforcing the dominant, narrow views of literacy. This critical reflection will prepare us to fight against policies that harm those who are most vulnerable, underrepresented, and disenfranchised.

I don't know much about Tyson. He showed up one week during a writing workshop, and I haven't seen him since, which hopefully means he somehow managed to escape the oppressive cycle of the juvenile justice system. The one night when Tyson was a part of the writing workshop, we were composing pantoum poems, which can be any length and in rhyme or blank verse, but it is made up of four-line stanzas repeated in this way:

1. (same as line 2)
2. (same as line 4)
3. (same as line 6)
4. (same as line 8)

Tyson's poem was fueled by hope, optimism, and pride. It is a reminder that when we listen to youths' voices and teach them to write, we provide them an opportunity to see their strengths, document their aspirations, and express hope for themselves and their futures.

1 My Name Will carry on
2 I will make of it what I can
3 Your name should tell a story
4 Even if people dont understand

5 (same as line 2)

6 People will surely Know

7 (same as line 4) That I was put on the earth

8 To shine bright and glow

9 (same as line 6) People will surely Know

10 I am what I cant show

11 (same as line 8) I will work exceedingly hard

12 So when Am gone my name
       Will Blow

Tyson's pantoum poem

References

Abrams, L., & Hyun, A. (2009). Mapping a process of negotiated identity among incarcerated male juvenile offenders. *Youth and Society, 41*(1), 26–52.

Afterschool Alliance. (2012). *Uncertain times: Afterschool programs still struggling in today's economy.* Retrieved from http://www.afterschoolalliance.org/documents/Uncertain_Times/Uncertain-Times-2012.pdf.

Anderson, M. (2015, October 29). Technology device ownership: 2015. *Pew Research Center.* Retrieved from http://www.pewinternet.org/2015/10/29/technology-device-ownership-2015.

Angelou, Maya. (1969). *I know why the caged bird sings.* New York: Random House.

Applebee, A., & Langer, J. (2009). What is happening in the teaching of writing? *English Journal, 98*(5), 18–28.

Applebee, A., & Langer, J. (2011). A snapshot of writing instruction in middle and high schools. *English Journal, 100*(6), 14–27.

Arts Council England. (2014). The value of arts and culture to people and society. Manchester, England.

Atwell, N. (1998). *In the middle: New understandings about writing, reading and learning.* Portsmouth, NH: Heinemann.

Austen, J. (1813/2017). *Pride and prejudice.* New York: Penguin Books.

Baca, J. (2002). *A place to stand.* New York: Grove Press.

Barton, D., & Hamilton, M. (1998). *Local literacies: Reading and writing in one community.* New York: Routledge.

Bauer, D. (2008). My entire football career. In J. Scieszka (ed.), *Guys write for guys read: Boys' favorite authors write about being boys* (pp. 33–35). New York: Viking.

Bazalgette, C., & Buckingham, D. (2013). Literacy, media and multimodality: A critical response. *Literacy, 47*(2), 95–102. Retrieved from https://doi.org/10.1111/j.1741-4369.2012.00666.x.

Benson, P. (2007). Developmental assets: An overview of theory, research, and practice. In R. K. Silbereisen & R. M. Lerner (eds.) *Approaches to positive youth development* (pp. 33–58). London: Sage.

Bernstein, N. (2014). *Burning down the house: The end of juvenile prison.* New York: The New Press.

Bluhm Legal Clinic. *Wrongful convictions of youth.* Retrieved from http://www.law.northwestern.edu/legalclinic/wrongfulconvictionsyouth/understandproblem/.

Boyd, D. (2013). *It's complicated: The social lives of networked teens.* New Haven, CT: Yale University Press.

Boyle, G. (2011). *Tattoos on the heart.* New York: Simon and Schuster.

Brinkley-Rubinstein, L., Craven, K. L., & McCormack, M. M. (2014). Shifting perceptions of race and incarceration as adolescents age: Addressing disproportionate minority contact by understanding how social environment informs racial attitudes. *Child and Adolescent Social Work Journal, 31*(1), 25–38.

Brown, T. (2007). Lost and turned out: Academic, social, and emotional experiences of students excluded from school. *Urban Education, 42*(5), 432–55.

Calkins, L. (1994). *The art of teaching writing*. Portsmouth, NH: Heinemann.

Chesney-Lind, M., & Shelden, R. (2004). *Girls, delinquency, and juvenile justice*. Belmont, CA: Thomson.

Christle, C., Nelson, M., & Jolivette, K. (2004). School characteristics related to the use of suspension. *Education and the Treatment of Children, 27*(4), 509–26.

Cochran-Smith, M., & Lytle, S. (eds.) (1993). *Inside/outside: Teacher research and knowledge*. New York: Teachers College Press.

College Entrance Examination Board. (2003). *The neglected "R": The need for a writing revolution: Report of the National Commission on Writing in America's Schools and Colleges*. New York: College Board. Retrieved from http://www.collegeboard.com/prod_downloads/writingcom/neglectedr.pdf.

Cope, B., & Kalantzis, M. (2009). "Multiliteracies": New literacies, new learning. *Pedagogies: An International Journal, 4*(3), 164–195.

Davies, B., & Harre, R. (1990). Positioning: The discursive production of selves. *Journal for the Theory of Social Behavior, 20*(1), 43–63.

Delpit, L. (1995/2006). *Other people's children: Cultural conflict in the classroom*. New York: The New Press.

Delpit, L. (2008). *The skin we speak*. New York: The New Press.

Dostoevsky, F. (1866/2012). *Crime and punishment*. Mineola, NY: Dover Publications.

Drakeford, W. (2002). The impact of an intensive literacy program to increase the literacy skills of youth confined in juvenile corrections. *Journal of Correctional Education, 53*(4), 32–42.

Dutro, E. (2013). Towards a pedagogy of the incomprehensible: Trauma and the imperative of critical witness in literacy classrooms. *Pedagogies: An International Journal, 8*(4), 301–15.

Emig, J. (1977). Writing as a mode of learning. *College Composition and Communication, 28*(2), 122–128.

Finders, M. (1997). *Just girls: Hidden literacies and life in junior high*. New York: Teachers College Press.

Fine, M. (1991). *Framing dropouts: Notes on the politics of an urban public high school*. New York: State University of New York Press.

Fine, M., Torre, M. E., Burns, A., & Payne, Y. (2007). Youth research/participatory methods for reform. In D. Thiessen & A. Cook-Sather (eds.), *International handbook of student experience in elementary and secondary school*. Dordrecht, the Netherlands: Springer.

Flower, L. (1979). Writer-based prose: A cognitive basis for problems in writing. *College English, 41*(1), 19–37.

Flower, L., & Hayes, J. (1981). A cognitive process theory of writing. *College Composition and Communication, 32*(4), 365–387.

Foley, R. (2001). Academic characteristics of incarcerated youth and correctional educational programs. *Journal of Emotional and Behavioral Disorders, 9*(4), 248–60.

Foucault, M. (1995). *Discipline and punish: The birth of prison*. New York: Vintage.

Gaiman, N. (2008). Why books are dangerous. In J. Scieszka (ed.), *Guys write for guys read: Boys' favorite authors write about being boys* (pp. 74–76). New York: Viking.

Gallagher, K. (2006). *Teaching adolescent writers*. Portland, ME: Stenhouse.

Gallagher, K. (2011). *Write like this: Teaching real-world writing through modeling and mentor texts*. Portland, ME: Stenhouse.

Gee, J. (2004). Language in the science classroom: Academic social languages as the heart of school-based literacy. In W. Saul (ed.), *Crossing borders in literacy and science instruction: Perspectives on theory and practice* (pp. 13–32). Arlington, VA: National Science Teachers Association.

Gooding, L. F. (2008). Finding your inner voice through song: Reaching adolescents with techniques common to poetry therapy and music therapy. *Journal of Poetry Therapy, 21*(4), 219–29.

Graham, S., Bruch, J., Fitzgerald, J., Friedrich, L., Furgeson, J., Greene, K., Kim, J., Lyskawa, J., Olson, C. B., & Smither Wulsin, C. (2016). Teaching secondary students to write effectively (NCEE 2017-4002). Washington, DC: National Center for Education Evaluation and Regional Assistance (NCEE), Institute of Education Sciences, U.S. Department of Education. https://ies.ed.gov/ncee/wwc/Docs/PracticeGuide/wwc_secondary_writing_110116.pdf

Graham, S., & Perin, D. (2007). *Writing next: Effective strategies to improve writing of adolescents in middle and high schools: A report to the Carnegie Corporation of New York.* Washington, DC: Alliance for Excellent Education. Retrieved from www.all4ed.org/files/WritingNext.pdf.

Graves, D. (1983). *Writing: Teachers and children at work.* Portsmouth, NH: Heinemann.

Greene, M. (1995). *Releasing the imagination: Essays on education, the arts, and social change.* San Francisco: Jossey-Bass.

Harris, P. J., Baltodano, H. M., Bal, A., Jolivette, K., & Malcahy, C. (2009). Reading achievement of incarcerated youth in three regions. *Journal of Correctional Education, 60,* 120–145.

Harste, J., Woodward, V., & Burke, C. (1984). *Language stories and literacy lessons.* Portsmouth, NH: Heinemann.

Heath, S. (1983). *Ways with words: Language, life and work in communities and classrooms.* Cambridge, England: Cambridge University Press.

Hinshaw, W. W., & Jacobi, T. (2015). What words might do: The challenge of representing women in prison and their writing. *Feminist Formations, 27*(1), 67–90.

Holman, B., & Ziedenberg, J. (2006). The dangers of detention. *Justice Policy Institute.* Retrieved from http://www.justicepolicy.org/images/upload/06-11_rep_dangersofdetention_jj.pdf.

Houchins, D. E., Jollvette, K., Krezmien, M. P., & Baltodano, H. M. (2008). A multi-state study examining the impact of explicit reading instruction with incarcerated students. *Journal of Correctional Education, 59*(1), 65–85.

Humes, E. (1996). *No matter how loud I shout: A year in the life of juvenile court.* New York: Simon & Schuster.

Ihanus, J. (2005). Touching stories in biblio-poetry therapy and personal development. *Journal of Poetry Therapy, 18*(2), 71–84.

Jacobi, T. (2011). Speaking out for social justice: The problem and possibilities of U.S. women's prison and jail writing workshops. *Critical Survey, 23*(3), 40–54.

Jewitt, C. (2008). Multimodality and literacy in school classrooms. *Review of Research in Education, 32,* 241–67.

Kirkland, D. (2013). A search past silence: The literacy of young black men. New York: Teachers College Press.

Kittle, P. (2008). *Write beside them.* Portsmouth, NH: Heinemann.

Kress, G. R., & van Leeuwen, T. (1996). *Reading images: The grammar of visual design.* London: Routledge.

Krisberg, B. (2005). *Juvenile justice: Redeeming our children.* Thousand Oaks, CA: Sage.

Langer, J. (2002). *Effective literacy instruction: Building successful reading and writing programs.* Urbana, IL: National Council of Teachers of English.

Leiber, M., & Fox, K. (2005). Race and the impact of detention on juvenile justice decision making. *Crime & Delinquency, 51*(4), 470–97.

Lenhart, A. (2015). *Teens, social media and technology overview 2015.* Pew Research Center. Retrieved from http://www.pewinternet.org/2015/04/09/teens-social-media-technology-2015/.

Lenhart, A., Arafeh, S., Smith, A., & Rankin Macgill, A. (2008). Teens, technology, and writing. Pew Internet and American Life Project, April 28, 2008. Retrieved from http://www.pewinternet.org/files/oldmedia//Files/Reports/2008/PIP_Writing_Report_FINAL3.pdf.pdf.

Leu, D. J., Kinzer, C. K., Coiro, J., Castek, J., & Henry, L. A. (2013). New literacies: A dual-level theory of the changing nature of literacy, instruction, and assessment. In D. E. Alvermann, N. J. Unrau, & R. B. Ruddell (eds.) *Theoretical models and processes of reading* (6th ed.). Newark, DE: International Reading Association.

Leve, L., Chamberlain, P., & Kim, H. (2015). Risks, outcomes, and evidence-based interventions for girls in the U.S. Juvenile Justice System. *Clinical Child Family Psychology Review, 18*(3), 252–279.

Liss, S. (2005). *No place for children.* Austin: University of Texas Press.

Malmgren, K. W., & Leone, P. E. (2000). Effects of a short-term auxiliary reading program on the reading skills of incarcerated youth. *Education and Treatment of Children, 23*(3), 239–247.

Mazza, N. (2003). *Poetry therapy: Theory and practice.* New York: Brunner-Routledge.

McAdams, D. (1993). *The stories we live by: Personal myths and the making of the self.* New York: Guilford Press.

McCarthy, S., & Moje, E. (2002). Identities matter. *Reading Research Quarterly, 37*(2), 228–238.

McWhorter, J. (2013, February). "Txtng is killing language. JK!!!" Video file. Retrieved from https://www.ted.com/talks/john_mcwhorter_txtng_is_killing_language_jk.

Mendez, L., Knoff, H., & Ferron, J. (2002). School demographic variables and out-of-school suspension rates: A quantitative and qualitative analysis of a large, ethnically diverse school district. *Psychology in the Schools, 39*(3), 259–77.

Mills, K. (2009). Multiliteracies: Interrogating competing discourses. *Language and Education, 23*(2), 103–116.

Milner, R., & Laughter, J. (2015). But good intentions are not enough: Preparing teachers to center race and poverty. *Urban Review* (47), 341–63.

Moje, E. (2000). "To be part of the story": The literacy practices of gangsta adolescents. *Teachers College Record, 102*(3), 651–90.

Moje, E. (2002). Re-framing adolescent literacy research for new times: Studying youth as a resource. *Reading Research and Instruction, 41*(3), 211–228.

Moll, L., Amanti, C., Neff, D., & Gonzalez, N. (1992). Funds of knowledge for teaching: Using a qualitative approach to connect homes and classrooms. *Theory into Practice, 31*(2), 132–141.

Moore, E., Gaskin, C., & Indig, D. (2013). Childhood maltreatment and post-traumatic stress disorder among incarcerated young offenders. *Child Abuse and Neglect,* 37, 861–70.

Morrell, E., (2008). *Critical literacy and urban youth: Pedagogies of access, dissent, and liberation.* New York: Routledge.

Murray, D. (1985). *A writer teaches writing.* Boston, MA: Houghton Mifflin Harcourt.

National Council of Teachers of English (2016, February). Professional knowledge for the teaching of writing. *NCTE Guideline.* Retrieved from http://www.ncte.org/positions/statements/teaching-writing.

Newell, G., Bloome, D., & Hirvela, A. (2015). *Teaching argumentative reading and writing in the high school English language arts classrooms.* New York: Routledge.

Newkirk, T., & Kent, R. (2007). *Teaching the neglected "R": Rethinking writing instruction in secondary classrooms.* Portsmouth, NH: Heinemann.

Nieto, S., & Bode, P. (2008). *Affirming diversity: The sociopolitical context of multicultural education.* Boston, MA: Allyn & Bacon.

Noguera, P. (2003). The trouble with black boys: The role and influence of environmental and cultural factors on the academic performance of African American males. *Urban Education, 38*(4), 431–59.

O'Connell, J. (2007). My sink-or-swim summer. *Best Life, 9*(9), 148.

Oppel, K. (2008). Anything can happen. In J. Scieszka (ed.), *Guys write for guys read: Boys' favorite authors write about being boys* (pp. 169–73). New York: Viking.

Pajares, F. (2003). Self-efficacy beliefs, motivation, and achievement in writing: A literature review. *Reading and Writing Quarterly,* 19, 139–58.

Pajares, F., Johnson, M., & Usher, E. (2007). Sources of writing self-efficacy beliefs of elementary, middle, and high school students. *Research in the Teaching of English, 42*(1), 104–20.

Piazza, C., & Siebert, C. (2008). Development and validation of a writing dispositions scale for elementary, middle, and high school students. *Journal of Educational Research, 101*(5), 275–85.

Prater, M. A., Johnstun, M. L., Dyches, T. T., & Johnstun, M. R. (2006). Using children's books as bibliotherapy for at-risk students: A guide for teachers. *Preventing School Failure, 50*(4), 5–13.

Purcell-Gates, V. (2007). Complicating the complex. In V. Purcell-Gates (ed.) *Cultural practices of literacy: Case studies of language, literacy, social practice, and power* (pp. 1–22). Mahwah, NJ: Lawrence Erlbaum Associates.

Purcell-Gates, V., Jacobson, E., & Degener, S. (2004). *Print literacy development: Uniting cognitive and social practice theories.* Cambridge, MA: Harvard University Press.

Pytash, K. E. (2013). "I'm a reader": Transforming incarcerated girls' lives in the English classroom. *English Journal, 102*(4), 67–73.

Pytash, K. E. (2014). "It's not simple": The complex literate lives of youth in a juvenile detention facility. In P. Dunston, L. Grambell, K. Headly, S. Fullerton, & P. Stecker (eds.) *63rd Yearbook of the Literacy Research Association* (pp. 216–228). Altamonte Springs, FL: Literacy Research Association.

Pytash, K. E. (2016). Girls on the fringe: The writing lives of two adolescent girls. *Reading and Writing Quarterly, 32*(4), 299–316.

Ray, K. (2006). *Study driven: A framework for planning units of study in the writing workshop.* Portsmouth, NH: Heinemann.

Rogers-Adkinson, D., Melloy, K., Stuart, S., Fletcher, L., & Rinaldi, C. (2008). Reading and written language competency of incarcerated youth. *Reading and Writing Quarterly, 24*, 197–218.

Samuelson, B. (2009). Ventriloquation in discussions of student writing: Examples from a high school English class. *Research in the Teaching of English, 44*(1), 52–88.

Sander, J. B., Patall, E. A., Amoscato, L. A., Fisher, A. L., & Funk, C. (2012). A meta-analysis of the effect of juvenile delinquency interventions on academic outcomes. *Children and Youth Services Review, 34*, 1695–1708.

Scieszka, J. (2008). Brothers. In J. Scieszka (ed.), *Guys write for guys read: Boys' favorite authors write about being boys* (pp. 214–16). New York: Viking.

Scieszka, J. (ed.), *Guys write for guys read: Boys' favorite authors write about being boys.* New York: Viking.

Scott, M., Underwood, M., & Lamis, D. (2015). Suicide and related behavior among youth involved in the juvenile justice system. *Child and Adolescent Social Work Journal, 32*, 517–27.

Search Institute. (2006). *Asset building.* Retrieved from http://ww2.nasbhc.org/RoadMap/CareManagement/Scope%20of%20Services/40%20Development%20Assets.pdf.

Sedlak, A. J., & McPherson, K. (2010). *Survey of youth in residential placement: Youth's needs and services. SYRP Report.* Rockville, MD: Westat.

Shakur, T. (2009). *The rose that grew from concrete.* New York: Pocket Books.

Shaughnessy, M. (1976). Diving in: An introduction to basic writing. *College Composition and Communication, 27*(3), 234–239.

Sixx, N. (2008). *Heroin diaries: A year in the life of a shattered rock star.* New York: Pocket Books.

Smagorinsky, P. (2008). *Teaching English by design: How to create and carry out instructional units.* Portsmouth, NH: Heinemann.

Smith, F. (1983). Reading like a writer. *Language Arts, 60*(5), 558–67.

Snyder, H., & Sickmund, M. (1999). *Juvenile offenders and victims: 1999 national report.* Washington, DC: Office of Juvenile Justice and Delinquency Prevention, U.S. Department of Justice.

Stanton, B. (2010). *Humans of New York.* Retrieved from http://www.humansofnewyork.com.

Tuck, E. (2009). Suspending damage: A letter to communities. *Harvard Educational Review,* *79*(3), 409–28. https://doi.org/10.17763/haer.79.3.n0016675661t3n15.

Turner, K. H., Abrams, S., Katic, E., & Donovan, M. J. (2014). Digitalk: The what and the why of adolescent digital language. *Journal of Literacy Research, 46*(2), 157–93.

Vacca, J. (2008). Crime can be prevented if schools teach juvenile offenders to read. *Children and Youth Services Review, 30*(9), 1055–1062.

Vidal, S., Prince, D., Connell, C. M., Caron, C. M., Kaufman, J. S., & Tebes, J. K. 2017. Maltreatment, family environment, and social risk factors: Determinants of the child welfare to juvenile justice transition among maltreated children and adolescents. *Child Abuse & Neglect 63*, 7–18.

White, M., & Epston, D. (1990). *Narrative means to therapeutic ends.* New York: Norton.

Winn, M. (2011). Girl time: Literacy, justice, and the school-to-prison pipeline. New York: Teachers College Press.

Wissman, K., & Wiseman, A. (2011). "That's my worst nightmare": Poetry and trauma in the middle school classroom. *Pedagogies: An International Journal, 6*(3), 234–49.

Wordes, M., Bynum, T., & Corley, C. (1994). Locking up youth: The impact of race on detention decisions. *Journal of Research in Crime and Delinquency, 31*(2), 149–65.

Wordes, M., & Jones, S. (1998). Trends in juvenile detention and steps toward reform. *Crime & Delinquency, 44*(4), 544–60.

About the Author

Kristine E. Pytash is an associate professor in teaching, learning, and curriculum studies at Kent State University's College of Education, Health, and Human Services, where she codirects the secondary integrated language arts teacher preparation program. She is a former high school English teacher. Her research focuses on the literacy practices of youth in alternative schools and juvenile detention facilities, and she studies disciplinary writing and how to prepare preservice teachers to teach writing. An underlying theme across all her lines of inquiry is how technology significantly influences young adults' literacy practices and their literacy instruction.